P9-BYN-390

QUESTIONS CHRISTIANS ASK

BIBLE STUDY GUIDE

From the Bible-teaching ministry of

Charles R. Swindoll

INSIGHT FOR LIVING

Charles R. Swindoll is a graduate of Dallas Theological Seminary and has served in pastorates since 1963, including churches in Texas, New England, and California. Since 1971 he has served as senior pastor of the First Evangelical Free Church of Fullerton, California. Chuck's radio program, "Insight for Living," began in 1979. In addition to his church and radio ministries, Chuck has authored numerous books and booklets on a variety of subjects.

Based on the outlines and transcripts of Chuck's sermons, the study guide text is coauthored by David Lien, a graduate of Westmont College and Dallas Theological Seminary. The Living Insights are written by Lee Hough, a graduate of the University of Texas at Arlington and Dallas Theological Seminary.

Editor in Chief:	**Director, Communications Division:**
Cynthia Swindoll	Carla Beck
Coauthor of Text:	**Project Manager:**
David Lien	Alene Cooper
Author of Living Insights:	**Project Supervisor:**
Lee Hough	Cassandra Clark
Assistant Editor:	**Art Director:**
Glenda Schlahta	Don Pierce
Copy Manager:	**Designer:**
Jac La Tour	Gary Lett
Copyediting Supervisor:	**Typographer:**
Marty Anderson	Bob Haskins
Copy Editor:	**Print Production Manager:**
Wendy Peterson	Deedee Snyder

An effort has been made to locate sources and obtain permission where necessary for the quotations used in this book. In the event of any unintentional omission, a modification will gladly be incorporated in future printings.

ISBN 0-8499-8405-X

Printed in the United States of America.

COVER PHOTOGRAPH: Owen Riss, Auguste Rodin's *The Thinker*

CONTENTS

INTRODUCTION

Throughout life there are questions that emerge in everyone's mind. Many of them come when we are children, and they don't stop during the adolescent years nor when we reach adulthood. But they do change. The older we get, the deeper our level of curiosity becomes . . . and the more crucial our concerns grow.

This is a study unlike any we have undertaken before. We are going to ask a dozen questions, and then allow the Scriptures to answer each one. Hopefully, you will find these questions on target and in touch. As we work our way through them, think about how they relate to your home, your work, your future, your life.

It is my prayer that God will use His Word not only to answer some of your questions but also to encourage and strengthen your heart. Let's pray together that lives will be changed as a result of these studies.

Chuck Swindoll

PUTTING TRUTH
INTO ACTION

K nowledge apart from application falls short of God's desire for
His children. He wants us to apply what we learn so that we
will change and grow. This study guide was prepared with these goals
in mind. As you go through the following pages, we hope your desire
to discover biblical truth will grow as your understanding of God's
Word increases, and that you will be encouraged to apply what
you've learned.

To assist you in your study, we've included a section called
Living Insights at the end of each lesson. These exercises will
challenge you to study further and to think of specific ways
to put your discoveries into action.

On occasion a lesson is followed by a ⚒ Digging Deeper section, which gives you additional information and resources to probe
further into some issues raised in that lesson.

There are many ways to use this guide—in personal devotions,
group studies, discussions with friends and family, and Sunday school
classes. And, of course, it's an ideal study aid when you're listening
to its corresponding "Insight for Living" radio series.

To benefit most from this study guide, we would encourage you
to consider it a spiritual journal. That's why we've included space
in the Living Insights for recording your thoughts and discoveries.
We hope you'll return to those sections often for review and encouragement as you continue to grow in your walk with Christ.

David Lien
Coauthor of Text

Lee Hough
Author of Living Insights

QUESTIONS
CHRISTIANS ASK

Chapter 1
WHO IS THIS JESUS?
Matthew 21:1–17

W e Christians are notorious for answering the wrong questions—
questions no one is asking. And when we do answer the right
questions, we do it in a way that is meaningless—we either fail to
identify with the struggles of the person or fail to answer in terms they
understand. Dr. Haddon Robinson is right on target when he says:

> A minister may stand before a congregation and deliver
> exegetically accurate sermons, scholarly and organized,
> but dead and powerless because they ignore the life-
> wrenching problems and questions of his hearers. Such
> sermons, spoken in a stained-glass voice using a code
> language never heard in the marketplace, dabble in
> great biblical concepts, but the audience feels that
> God belonged to the long ago and far away. Expositors
> must not only answer the questions our fathers asked;
> they must wrestle with the questions our children ask.
> Men or women who speak effectively for God must
> first struggle with the questions of their age and then
> speak to those questions from the eternal truth of God.[1]

We need to take time to answer a few of the more significant
questions people are asking. And many of those questions have to
do with the identity of Jesus. Who is He? Why did He come? What
did He teach? How can I connect with Him? These questions are
the same ones asked centuries ago by people who lived when Jesus
did. Let's see how they were answered then.

---

1. Haddon W. Robinson, *Biblical Preaching* (Grand Rapids, Mich.: Baker Book House,
1980), pp. 77–78.

Some Background Information

Matthew 21 opens the curtain on the final act in the drama of Jesus' life, one week before the Crucifixion.

What's happening?

It's Passover, the single most significant season of celebration in Jewish life. Jerusalem is packed with people for this most important of Jewish festivals, the Feast of Unleavened Bread.[2] This year their Messiah is in their midst, but the irony is that they don't even know it.

Who's around?

There are three basic groups of people crowding into Jerusalem. First, there are Jesus and His most intimate followers (v. 1a). There is also a group of people referred to as "the multitudes" who make up the broader base of Jesus' followers—people who have heard Him teach and seen Him perform miracles (v. 9). A third group of people, the majority of the crowd, knows nothing about Christ (v. 10).

An Unusual Celebration

Jesus' journey toward Jerusalem takes Him along a dusty little ribbon of road from Bethany through Bethphage, over the crest of the Mount of Olives. Just before He reaches the city, He pauses to give His disciples some last-minute instructions.

Jesus and His Disciples

The disciples' minds are probably on the teeming city as they anticipate their arrival, their ears filled with the cacophony of sounds ricocheting up and down the Kidron Valley. But Jesus' mind is on formulating a plan. And He breaks the rhythm of their thoughts with this command.

> "Go into the village opposite you, and immediately you
> will find a donkey tied there and a colt with her; untie
> them, and bring them to Me." (v. 2)

He stills the question on their lips with a response for anyone who questions their behavior.

> "If anyone says something to you, you shall say, 'The
> Lord has need of them,' and immediately he will send
> them." (v. 3)

---

2. The Feast of Unleavened Bread is synonymous with Passover (see *The Zondervan Pictorial Encyclopedia of the Bible* [Grand Rapids, Mich.: Zondervan Publishing House, 1976], vol. 2, p. 523).

Jesus' directions seem spontaneous, but centuries of prophecy are unfolding in this moment. Jesus' finger is on the page of Scripture where Zechariah had predicted this day (see Zech. 9:9), and his words are about to be fulfilled.

> Now this took place that what was spoken through the prophet might be fulfilled, saying,
> "Say to the daughter of Zion,
> 'Behold your King is coming to you,
> Gentle, and mounted on a donkey,
> Even on a colt, the foal of a beast of
> burden.'" (Matt. 21:4–5)

Zechariah must have scratched his head puzzling over the King of Israel riding on a donkey instead of a white horse—and so must the disciples. Yet the prophet wrote it down, and now the disciples are helping carry it out.

> And the disciples went and did just as Jesus had directed them, and brought the donkey and the colt, and laid on them their garments, on which He sat. (vv. 6–7)

Messiah and His Multitudes

Has there ever been a more eloquent contrast than a king riding humbly on a beast of burden known for its stubbornness and stupidity? No blare of trumpets, no regal robes, no jeweled crown. But there are many in the crowd who put two and two together.

> And most of the multitude spread their garments in the road, and others were cutting branches from the trees, and spreading them in the road. (v. 8)

And all the while they proclaim in unison,

> "Hosanna[3] to the Son of David;
> Blessed is He who comes in the name of the Lord;
> Hosanna in the highest!" (v. 9b)

But not everyone recognizes Him. Amongst shouts of joy, some are silent. Mouths drop open in surprise or twist into frowns of confusion as the strange little parade passes by.

The Savior and the City

Don't miss a little word tucked into verse 10.

---

3. *Hosanna* means "Save, we pray!" This expression comes from Psalm 118:25–27.

3

And when He had entered Jerusalem, all the city was *stirred*, saying, "Who is this?" And the multitudes were saying, "This is the prophet Jesus, from Nazareth in Galilee." (vv. 10–11, emphasis added)

We get our word *seismic* from the Greek term translated "stirred." Jesus' entry causes no small commotion! News of His arrival rumbles like an earthquake through the city, sending aftershocks in all directions. The people aren't simply asking the identity of the man on the donkey—the implication of their question is, Who does this guy think he is, anyway? In fact, some of the Pharisees urge Him, "Teacher, rebuke Your disciples" (Luke 19:39). In other words, "Tell them who you *really* are! Tell them you're just a carpenter's son from Nazareth!"

But Jesus meets their eyes and says simply,

"I tell you, if these become silent, the stones will cry out!" (v. 40)

The Lord and the Temple

Jesus doesn't defend Himself. He doesn't rebuke the people who don't recognize Him. He just heads for the temple—to do a little housecleaning.[4]

And Jesus entered the temple and cast out all those who were buying and selling in the temple, and overturned the tables of the moneychangers and the seats of those who were selling doves. And He said to them, "It is written, 'My house shall be called a house of prayer'; but you are making it a robbers' den." (Matt. 21:12–13)

Jesus isn't all zealous anger. He's a conqueror, all right, but He's a gentle conqueror. G. Campbell Morgan comments on what happens next.

Then for one brief moment, so brief a moment that if we are not careful we miss it in our reading—we find the Temple made beautiful indeed; "the blind and the lame came to Him in the Temple, and He healed them." That was one brief moment of restoration. For one brief moment the house was no longer a den of robbers, it was a house of prayer. What a picture! The

4. This is Jesus' second cleansing of the temple. The first time is recorded in John 2:13–22, and it took place earlier in His ministry.

Temple was not tidy. There were overturned tables, and money scattered everywhere, the débris of a great reconstruction. But there were the blind and the lame; and the face that a moment before had flamed with indignation was soft with the radiance of a great pity. That is one of the greatest pictures in the Gospel according to Matthew. He casts out, but He takes in; He overthrows, but He builds up.[5]

That should have been enough. They should have known who He was after that. But the chief priests and scribes trample right through the healing and right up to Jesus. And they rebuke Him.

But when the chief priests and the scribes saw the wonderful things that He had done, and the children who were crying out in the temple and saying, "Hosanna to the Son of David," they became indignant, and said to Him, "Do You hear what these are saying?" (vv. 15–16a)

Jesus calmly directs them to their own Scriptures.

And Jesus said to them, "Yes; have you never read, 'Out of the mouth of infants and nursing babes Thou hast prepared praise for Thyself'?" (v. 16b)

Jesus is quoting from Psalm 8. He could put their backs to the wall if He goes on to quote the rest of that passage: "Because of Thine adversaries, / To make the enemy and the revengeful cease." But He doesn't. That tough, gentle man knows that rebuking a scoffer never wins him over (Prov. 9:7).

So instead, Jesus leaves them alone. As swiftly as He had entered the temple, He turns and walks out, leaving them with their thoughts and what they have seen, and He goes to an unnamed place in Bethany (Matt. 21:17).

A Timely Question

The question we began with was, "Who is this Jesus?"

This is no idle question to be answered superficially. It's one of the most crucial questions anyone can ask. Our study today gives us four answers.

First: *Jesus is a courageous man.* It took courage to ride into a city where He would face hostile people. It took courage to stand alone

5. G. Campbell Morgan, *The Gospel According to Matthew* (New York, N.Y.: Fleming H. Revell Co., 1929), p. 252.

and clean up the temple. This is no pale, Milquetoast Savior, but a man who bravely faced not just the temple, but the Cross.

Second: *Jesus is a humble king.* He did not demand a chariot and royal treatment. He wasn't offended because many didn't know who He was. He didn't play up to the powerful, but took time to heal the least powerful—the blind and the lame.

Third: *Jesus is a patient Lord.* He was willing to wait for His crown. He quietly endured abuse from those who disliked Him, and He accepted their misunderstanding of His motives.

Fourth: *Jesus is the sinner's Savior.* Some people resented Jesus' barging in on their business, so they rejected Him. Others gave Him praise, sought His healing, and shouted "Hosanna!"

Jesus slips into our lives today as well—sometimes quietly, riding humbly on a donkey; sometimes compassionately, reaching out to heal. But sometimes He strides in in anger, overturning the tables in our lives with roughness and shouting.

And then He leaves us alone to think.

What do you think about this Jesus? Are you confused by a king who passes by so humbly and unpretentiously? Are you angry and resentful because He upsets your life? Or do you welcome Him with fronds of praise and seek Him as your Savior and King?

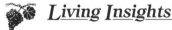 *Living Insights* STUDY ONE

Who is this Jesus?

In the catalog of crucial questions, the answer to this one stands alone as the cornerstone upon which all others build. Let's linger a moment over the answer by comparing the profile of Jesus drawn in Matthew 21 to the one of Christ at the Cross.

Carefully reread the definition for each characteristic that came at the end of this lesson, read the corresponding passage listed here, and, finally, note the similarities between the two.

The Jesus of Matthew 21   **The Jesus at the Cross**

Jesus is a courageous man.   Matthew 26:36–45

_____

_____

Jesus is a humble king.   John 18:28–38, Luke 22:49–51

_____

_____

_____

Jesus is a patient Lord.   Matthew 26:47–56

_____

_____

_____

Jesus is a sinner's Savior.   Luke 23:39–43

_____

_____

_____

C. S. Lewis, in his book *Mere Christianity*, shows us what our options are in answering for ourselves the question "Who is Christ?"

> I am trying here to prevent anyone saying the really foolish thing that people often say about Him: "I'm ready to accept Jesus as a great moral teacher, but I don't accept His claim to be God." That is the one thing we must not say. A man who was merely a man and said the sort of things Jesus said would not be a great moral teacher. He would either be a lunatic—on a level with the man who says he is a poached egg—or else he would be the Devil of Hell. You must make your choice. Either this man was, and is, the Son of God: or else a madman or something worse.[6]

6. C. S. Lewis, *Mere Christianity*, rev. and enl. (New York, N.Y.: Macmillan Publishing Co., 1952), pp. 55–56.

Take some time to answer the question Jesus put to His own disciples in Mark 8:29, "But who do you say that I am?" Use the space provided to write down your thoughts.

_____

_____

_____

_____

_____

_____

_____

_____

_____

_____

_____

_____

_____

_____

_____

Living Insights

The Passover masses were shaken by the seismic tremor that emanated from the question on everyone's lips, "Who is this Jesus?"

In response to that question, this lesson paints four portraits of Christ from Matthew 21:1–17. Remember what they are? The courageous man, the humble king, the patient Lord, and the sinner's Savior.

According to Romans 8:29, God desires all believers to be transformed into living portraits of Christ. So take a moment now to see if His silhouette is emerging in your life. Review the portraits of Christ that follow; then think through the corresponding questions. Finally, paint a word picture of yourself by checking the appropriate boxes in the right-hand column.

Portraits of Christ

Courageous Man	
Question	Self-Portrait
Do I have the courage to enter the hostile marketplace of humanity and make a stand, alone if necessary?	☐ Committed Disciple ☐ Searching Follower ☐ Part of the Masses
Humble King	
Question	Self-Portrait
Is an attitude of humility reflected in my actions—do I serve or seek to be served?	☐ Committed Disciple ☐ Searching Follower ☐ Part of the Masses
Patient Lord	
Question	Self-Portrait
How patiently did I respond the last time I felt the sharp point of someone's critical tongue?	☐ Committed Disciple ☐ Searching Follower ☐ Part of the Masses
Sinner's Savior	
Question	Self-Portrait
Am I willingly sacrificing so that the lost might know Christ through me?	☐ Committed Disciple ☐ Searching Follower ☐ Part of the Masses

Unfortunately, many of us may end up feeling more like a pencil sketch of Christ than a masterpiece. However, remember Paul's words in Philippians 1:6 and be encouraged to press on!

> For I am confident of this very thing, that He who began a good work in you will perfect it until the day of Christ Jesus.

Chapter 2

CHRIST IS RAISED, BUT WHAT ABOUT ME?

1 Corinthians 15:12–57

Tombstones are the silent markers of life past. Their epitaphs are final summaries of people's lives. Some are profound, some tragic, a few philosophical, a handful even humorous. Like this one, found in England.

> Beneath this stone, a lump of clay,
> Lies Arabella Young;
> Who, on the twenty-fourth of May,
> Began to hold her tongue.

Or this one, in a windy Kansas prairie:

> I told you I was sick!

In his immortal work on Christian martyrs, John Foxe exhumes a few remarks found on the gravestones of slain saints. "Here lies Marcia, put to rest in a dream of peace." And "Victorious in peace and in Christ." Epitaphs you might see in any graveyard . . . except these were engraved in the context of persecution. Compare their hopeful message to the despair of the non-Christian.

> Live for the present hour, since we are sure of nothing else.

> Traveler, curse me not as you pass, for I am in darkness and cannot answer.[1]

Christian or not, hopeful or despairing, we all have in common the inevitableness of death. But once death comes, our paths divide.

Hope Is a Dividing Line among Epitaphs

People have always wondered about death . . . and especially about life after death. Even Job once asked, "If a man dies, will he live again?" (Job 14:14a).

---

1. *Fox[e]'s Book of Martyrs*, ed. William Byron Forbush (Grand Rapids, Mich.: Zondervan Publishing House, 1954), pp. 11–12.

Death is difficult for anyone to face. In the New Testament, we see that Martha, Lazarus' sister, was no exception. Theoretically, Martha believed in resurrection, but practically, she was overwhelmed by her brother's early death and Jesus' apparent unconcern. So in her grief and disappointment, she confronts Jesus.

"Lord, if You had been here, my brother would not have died." (John 11:21b)

Jesus assures her that Lazarus will rise again, and as He does, He puts a crucial piece of that eternal puzzle into place.

Jesus said to her, "Your brother shall rise again." Martha said to Him, "I know that he will rise again in the resurrection on the last day."[2] Jesus said to her, "I am the resurrection and the life; he who believes in Me shall live even if he dies, and everyone who lives and believes in Me shall never die. Do you believe this?" (vv. 23–26)

Jesus' words give the believer a hope that the unbeliever can never have. Joseph Bayly, in his book *The View from a Hearse*, gives us a stark picture of the dividing line between hope and desolation. Waiting to thank the doctor who had been so kind to his little boy as he was dying, Bayly offered hope to a woman whose small son was also dying.

"It's good to know, isn't it," I spoke slowly, choosing my words with unusual care, "that even though the medical outlook is hopeless, we can have hope for our children in such a situation. We can be sure that after our child dies, he'll be completely removed from sickness and suffering and everything like that, and be completely well and happy."

"If I could only believe that," the woman replied. "But I don't. When he dies, I'll just have to cover him up with dirt and forget I ever had him."[3]

Many people in tragic circumstances have no sense of hope beyond death. It is a horrible way to live—and a horrible way to die.

Fortunately, it's not the only way.

---

2. Martha's grief had to do with the pain of bereavement, not a denial of the promised resurrection. She had hope in resurrection, but was hurt that Jesus had not kept her brother from dying. Jesus resuscitated Lazarus (vv. 43–44); however, he did die again and now awaits the resurrection that Martha refers to in verse 24.

3. Joseph Bayly, *The View from a Hearse* (Elgin, Ill.: David C. Cook Publishing Co., 1969), p. 13. This book has since been retitled *The Last Thing We Talk About*.

Jesus' Resurrection Gives Hope

Our link to life after death is Jesus' own Resurrection. If Jesus has been raised from the dead, then resurrection is indeed possible. As Paul says,

> Now if Christ is preached, that He has been raised from the dead, how do some among you say that there is no resurrection of the dead? (1 Cor. 15:12)

And it's His Resurrection that gives us hope.

Jesus Himself has risen from the dead.

We can't deny history's record—the Bible gives the evidence, and changed lives prove it true.[4] But for the sake of argument, let's suppose with Paul that Christ never rose.

> But if there is no resurrection of the dead, not even Christ has been raised; and if Christ has not been raised, then our preaching is vain, your faith also is vain. Moreover we are even found to be false witnesses of God, because we witnessed against God that He raised Christ, whom He did not raise, if in fact the dead are not raised. For if the dead are not raised, not even Christ has been raised; and if Christ has not been raised, your faith is worthless; you are still in your sins. Then those also who have fallen asleep in Christ have perished. If we have hoped in Christ in this life only, we are of all men most to be pitied. (vv. 13–19)

Pull out the Resurrection from the story of Christ, and the elements of our faith fall like dominoes. If Christ wasn't raised, then not only will we die, but we'll die in our sins.

But Christ was raised. And no longer do we have to die in our sins or resign ourselves to death.

Since Jesus rose, Christians, too, will rise.

Paul continues his train of logical thought.

> But now Christ has been raised from the dead, the first fruits of those who are asleep. For since by a man came death, by a man also came the resurrection of the dead. For as in Adam all die, so also in Christ all

---

4. For further study of the historical proof of Jesus' Resurrection, see *Evidence That Demands a Verdict,* by Josh McDowell (San Bernardino, Calif.: Here's Life Publishers, 1979).

shall be made alive. But each in his own order: Christ
the first fruits, after that those who are Christ's at His
coming. (vv. 20–23)

The connection between Jesus' Resurrection and the believer's
resurrection cannot be minimized. As William Barclay explains:

The first-fruits were a sign of the harvest to come; and
the Resurrection of Jesus was a sign of the resurrection
of all believers which was to come.[5]

**Since we will be entering an imperishable heaven, we'll need
an imperishable body.**

As we enter immortality, our mortal bodies must be changed.

As is the earthy, so also are those who are earthy; and
as is the heavenly, so also are those who are heavenly.
And just as we have borne the image of the earthy,
we shall also bear the image of the heavenly. Now I
say this, brethren, that flesh and blood cannot inherit
the kingdom of God; nor does the perishable inherit
the imperishable. (vv. 48–50)

For some, the metamorphosis will occur after death. Others will
experience it at the coming of Christ.

Behold, I tell you a mystery; we shall not all sleep, but
we shall all be changed, in a moment, in the twinkling
of an eye, at the last trumpet; for the trumpet will
sound, and the dead will be raised imperishable, and
we shall be changed. (vv. 51–52)

The last generation of Christians living when Jesus returns are
invited to a picnic nowhere near a cemetery or a hospital, to a place
where no one remembers any tears or disease or pain or death. They
will bypass the grave and go straight to heaven, to a magnificent
family reunion and a home with Christ forever.

If you want to be resurrected, there is a way.

German theologian Helmut Thielicke passes along Jesus' invitation to a resurrected life.

The Easter faith, then, is not just an upward glance
to satisfy my curiosity about the mysterious hereafter.
It is a summons of the Prince of Life to the present

5. William Barclay, *The Letters to the Corinthians*, rev. ed., The Daily Study Bible
Series (Philadelphia, Pa.: Westminster Press, 1975), p. 150.

13

hour of life: "Be reconciled to God; seize the new life which is offered; bury your old man in the grave where Jesus lay. Now is the accepted time; now His arms are open to you; now the Master is seeking companions."[6]

Since Jesus has been raised, there is hope in the midst of tragedy.

It's amazing how the hope of resurrection changes our perspective. Where we once felt despair, we now feel joy and relief. Not even death can steal hope's power.

"O death, where is your victory? O death, where is your sting?" The sting of death is sin, and the power of sin is the law; but thanks be to God, who gives us the victory through our Lord Jesus Christ. (vv. 55–57)

And that is the greatest epitaph of all.

In the shadow of the cemetery, when death's darkness threatens to overwhelm us, there is always one bright hope.

Do you know that source of hope? Have you seen it shining through your darkest nights? That hope cost Jesus His life. But it's there for you, dispelling the shadows and offering you eternal life.

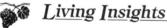 *Living Insights* STUDY ONE

An important aspect of good Bible study is correlation, which deals with how the Scriptures interrelate. It has been said that no man is an island—and it could just as well be said that no thought or verse is an island either. What we believe in one area will always carry with it consequences in others. Dr. Larry Crabb provides an excellent example of this in his book *Effective Biblical Counseling,* which presents some modern psychologists' attempts to eliminate man's responsibility for sin.

Eliminate responsibility and you do away with guilt. Do away with guilt and sin no longer exists. With the removal of sin the cross of Christ becomes a religious martyrdom rather than the basis of redemption.[7]

6. From *Twenty Centuries of Great Preaching: An Encyclopedia of Preaching,* by Clyde E. Fant, Jr., and William M. Pinson, Jr. (Waco, Tex.: Word Books, 1971), vol. 12, p. 276.

7. Lawrence J. Crabb, Jr., *Effective Biblical Counseling* (Grand Rapids, Mich.: Zondervan Publishing House, 1977), p. 42.

As we saw in our lesson, Paul lists some important consequences of denying the resurrection of the dead (1 Cor. 15:12–19). But let's take this thought progression backwards. Start by changing verse 19 into a positive declaration: "Christ is raised! Christians of all people are most to be envied." Make your way back up through verse 12, reversing each negative statement and making it a positive one. Write your version in the space below.

_____

_____

_____

_____

_____

_____

_____

_____

_____

_____

_____

You have just written a very profound declaration of your faith and hope!

🍇 Living Insights

Like Simon Peter did when Christ was crucified, most of us have felt our hope ebb at times; and in its place seep disillusionment, loneliness, hurt. Is it possible we have never really stopped to consider our Christian basis for hope and how it should affect our lives?

Let's do that now by addressing some personal issues. Before each of the following questions a quote has been given to spark your

thinking. Take a moment to reflect on these quotes before writing
your response.

>Loneliness.
>It's a cry. A moan, a wail. It's a gasp whose origin
>is the recesses of our souls.
>Can you hear it? The abandoned child. The divor-
>cée. The quiet home. The empty mailbox. The long
>days. The longer nights. A one-night stand. A for-
>gotten birthday. A silent phone.[8]

In my moments of loneliness, am I able to hope in Christ? Or
is my hope hobbled by conditions I attach to it: "I'll exhibit hope
in you, Lord, *if* you give me this husband, wife, these friends . . . "?

_____

_____

_____

Is my hope in life based on the resurrected Christ; or is it bal-
anced on the thin wire of bank accounts, status, friends?

_____

_____

◆

>The most gut-wrenching cry of loneliness in history
>came not from a prisoner or a widow or a patient. It
>came from a hill, from a cross, from a Messiah.
>"My God, my God!" he screamed. "Why did you
>abandon me!"
>Never have words carried so much hurt. Never has
>one being been so lonely.[9]

Is it unspiritual for me to say I have hope in Christ and yet still
experience pain?

_____

_____

_____

8. Max Lucado, *No Wonder They Call Him the Savior* (Portland, Oreg.: Multnomah
Press, 1986), p. 45.
9. Lucado, *Savior*, p. 47.

How can my hope of a future resurrection affect me today?

_____

_____

_____

_____

I keep thinking of all the people who cast despairing eyes toward the dark heavens and cry "Why?"

And I imagine him. I imagine him listening. I
picture his eyes misting and a pierced hand brushing
away a tear. And although he may offer no answer,
although he may solve no dilemma, although the question may freeze painfully in mid-air, he who also was
once alone, understands.[10]

Blessed be the God and Father of our Lord Jesus Christ,
who according to His great mercy has caused us to be
born again to a *living hope through the resurrection of
Jesus Christ from the dead.* (emphasis added)

What's this? Another quote from some theologian in an ivory
tower who has never gone through real pain like I have?

No, it's from Simon Peter (1 Pet. 1:3).

10. Lucado, *Savior*, p. 48.

17

Chapter 3

HOW CAN I WIN OVER WORRY?

Luke 10:38–42, Isaiah 40:27–31,
Matthew 6:24–34, Philippians 4:4–7

T his chapter is dedicated to all the Marthas of the world. Not literally all the women named Martha, but all the people cut from the same pattern as the Martha in the Bible. Modern-day Marthas can be anyone: male or female, young or old, rich or poor, married or single, new Christians or veteran saints. But one thing is sure—an anxious cloud hovers over their heads and fogs their hearts.

We all know what worry is. It's when we pay the interest on trouble before the bill comes due. As someone once put it, worry is like "a thin stream of fear trickling through the mind. If encouraged, it cuts a channel into which all other thoughts are drained."[1]

Biblical Analysis of Worry

Let's get a closer view of worry by paying a visit to the home of that biblical Martha on the same day that Jesus is visiting.

As we walk through the door, a definite flurry of flustered activity confronts us. It seems Jesus' presence has caused an unusual stir.

> Now as they were traveling along, [Jesus] entered a certain village; and a woman named Martha welcomed Him into her home. And she had a sister called Mary, who moreover was listening to the Lord's word, seated at His feet. But Martha was distracted with all her preparations; and she came up to Him, and said, "Lord, do You not care that my sister has left me to do all the serving alone? Then tell her to help me." (Luke 10:38–40)

We can't help but smile with understanding. Here is a responsible, conscientious woman, determined to have everything just right in honor of Jesus' visit. But Mary, her sister, leaves her with all the preparations. And on top of this, it seems to Martha that Jesus hasn't

---

1. A. S. Roche, in *Quote Unquote*, comp. Lloyd Cory (Wheaton, Ill.: SP Publications, Victor Books, 1977), p. 378.

even noticed she is struggling in the kitchen all alone. Caught up in her worried busyness, Martha gets irritated not only with Mary but with Jesus as well. So the Lord gently rebukes her,

> "Martha, Martha, you are worried and bothered about so many things; but only a few things are necessary, really only one, for Mary has chosen the good part, which shall not be taken away from her." (vv. 41–42)

The Greek term for *worry* means "to be divided" or "inwardly distracted." Jesus was saying, "Martha, you are all torn up inside." The origin of our English word *worry* gives us an even clearer picture of what Martha must have been feeling.

> At first glance there seems to be little connection between the physical act of "strangling" and the mental process of "worrying." However, the word "worry" is derived from the old German word *wurgen* meaning "to choke." Somehow, by extension, the term came to be used to denote "mental strangulation" . . . and then, to describe the condition of being harrassed with anxiety or care.[2]

Anxiety over details had strangled Martha's ability to see the larger picture. Worry chokes us, too, in several ways.

The Faces Worry Wears

A worried face is a wrinkled one. Look at the different contortions worry can produce.

First, there is the face of *anger and impatience*. As they did with Martha, these feelings rush in where there is an absence of inner tranquility; when we've run out of rest and confidence in God.

Second, there's the face of *rush and hurry*. Like Martha, who was too busy for her own guest, we become frantic with our own busyness. Instead of moving through life at a leisurely pace, we ricochet off the walls.

Third, *fear and panic* contort our countenance, sometimes with serious results. An article in *Newsweek* magazine reported that a woman stayed in her home from age 31 until age 61 because she was afraid to go outside.[3] It's easy to become so panic-stricken that we can't think rationally.

2. *Quote Unquote*, p. 378.
3. "The Fight to Conquer Fear," *Newsweek*, April 23, 1984, p. 66.

Worry's last face is wrinkled with *pessimism and criticism*. When Martha lashed out, her critical spirit launched a manipulative campaign soliciting Jesus' sympathy—"Lord, do You not care?" Worry twists our faces with gloom, pessimism, and blame.

The Damage Worry Produces

Spiritually, worry assaults our faith, and we end up in a fog of doubt that blurs the face of God. Physically, it steals our health— many of the medical problems that ravage our bodies are stress-induced. Emotionally, it destroys our peace; the tranquility necessary for a normal life evaporates.

Divine Alternatives to Worry

When a storm is on the horizon, we often search for shelter of our own instead of for rest in God's Word. And far too many of us blame our humanness for such misplaced focus. We excuse, analyze, discuss, rationalize, and allow our feelings to control us rather than discipline ourselves to listen to what God says.

How can we abandon worry? We can begin by considering three alternatives. These are not new. They do not rhyme. And they won't seem profound or scientific or clever. But they are all biblical, and they all work.

A Willingness to Wait

Think back on a time when you thought God was keeping Himself hidden from you, or when you felt He was not interested in defending you against injustice. A whole nation once felt like that— the nation of Israel. Isaiah sums up their feelings.

> Why do you say, O Jacob, and assert, O Israel,
> "My way is hidden from the Lord,
> And the justice due me escapes the notice of my God"?
> (Isa. 40:27)

These are the words of worriers. But Isaiah responds with words of comfort.

> Do you not know? Have you not heard?
> The Everlasting God, the Lord, the Creator of the
> ends of the earth
> Does not become weary or tired.
> His understanding is inscrutable. (v. 28)

The prophet says, in effect, "Allow me to brush the dust off some basic theology so that your questions may be answered!" He is encouraging them to remember the significance of God's names: Everlasting God, Lord, Creator. He wants them to climb to a different vantage point, to see things from God's point of view. The title "Everlasting God" encompasses all time and beyond—infinity. "Lord" implies total control, even of difficult circumstances. And "Creator" depicts God as the Master Architect, planner of each individual and each situation. The good news is that God doesn't hoard His power and understanding. Rather, He dispenses it to those who submit to His gracious hand.

> He gives strength to the weary,
> And to him who lacks might He increases power.
> (v. 29)

We do not have the strength to handle life by ourselves—even young and strong people buckle under its pressures. Renewal escapes us as long as we determine to work harder, run faster, outfox, or intimidate those who oppose us. Would you like to exchange a hassled, drained life for one of new strength? Rejuvenation occurs when we decide to wait upon God's strength rather than lean on our own.

> Though youths grow weary and tired,
> And vigorous young men stumble badly,
> Yet those who wait for the Lord
> Will *gain* new strength;
> They will mount up with wings like eagles,
> They will run and not get tired,
> They will walk and not become weary.
> (vv. 30–31, emphasis added)

The word *gain* in Hebrew suggests making an exchange—of weakness for strength, worry for rest. Of course, waiting on God does not necessarily mean sitting back and doing nothing—but sometimes it does. Be willing to wait for God, especially when you have exhausted your own supply of strength and wisdom.

A Commitment to Christ

Our first alternative to worry is waiting. Another alternative is commitment to Christ.

The last eleven verses of Matthew 6 include five references to being anxious. This is a passage we'd be wise to study! In it, we find our second clue to avoiding worry.

The Greek term for *anxious* gives the idea of being "distracted, preoccupied, vexed." In this passage Jesus wants us to see the setting that produces these negative emotions.

"No one can serve two masters; for either he will hate the one and love the other, or he will hold to one and despise the other. You cannot serve God and mammon." (v. 24)

People who are pulled from two different sides are eventually pulled apart, or else one side wins over the other. Jesus understands that we are tempted to make material resources our security, and He knows that God's place is often preempted by riches. But the fact remains that that tug-of-war only disrupts our peace, and reliance on money creates worries instead of relieving them. Our material resources are gifts to be wisely managed. They were never designed to be an antidote for anxiety.

Jesus goes on to offer us comfort when we encounter bothersome issues, like a concern about life's essentials.

"For this reason I say to you, do not be anxious for your life, as to what you shall eat, or what you shall drink; nor for your body, as to what you shall put on. Is not life more than food, and the body than clothing?" (v. 25)

Instead of fretting, look at other parts of creation, like the birds. They are cared for, and you are certainly worth more than they (v. 26).

We also worry about things we cannot change.

"And which of you by being anxious can add a single cubit to his life's span?" (v. 27)

Adding a cubit to life's span may refer to our height or how long we live. In either case, Jesus encourages us to accept what has been dealt us physically.

A third worry many of us have relates to our appearance.

"And why are you anxious about clothing? Observe how the lilies of the field grow; they do not toil nor do they spin, yet I say to you that even Solomon in all his glory did not clothe himself like one of these. But if God so arrays the grass of the field, which is alive today and tomorrow is thrown into the furnace, will He not much more do so for you, O men of little faith?" (vv. 28–30)

In all our worries, Jesus reminds us to see things as God sees them. That is the key—and if we fail to grasp it, the thought of tomorrow can cause us unnecessary grief.

"Do not be anxious for tomorrow; for tomorrow will care for itself. Each day has enough trouble of its own." (v. 34)

Just handle today. If today is Sunday, deal with all that Sunday presents to you, without worrying ahead to Monday. Plan for the future, but live in the present. There is enough to sort out today without dealing with the phantom of tomorrow.

All of us face the temptation to rely on our own resources, possessions, and financial security to get us through. And Jesus, knowing this, rebukes us strongly.

"Do not be anxious then, saying, 'What shall we eat?' or 'What shall we drink?' or 'With what shall we clothe ourselves?' For all these things the Gentiles eagerly seek; for your heavenly Father knows that you need all these things." (vv. 31–32)

There is only one thing worth our preoccupation and attention.

"But seek first His kingdom and His righteousness; and all these things shall be added to you." (v. 33)

Seek His kingdom, where He is ruler; and pursue His righteousness, since He is the giver. "All these things"—food and clothing—will come. Not in the manner or quantity we expect, maybe, but they will come nonetheless. Our worry will diminish when we cease relying on our own resources.

A Priority of Prayer

Instead of relying on our own strength, we are to wait. Instead of trusting in our possessions, we are to trust Christ. Instead of depending solely on others' counsel, we are to make prayer a priority. In Philippians 4, Paul gives us three commands to help ward off worry.

Rejoice in the Lord always; again I will say, rejoice! Let your forbearing spirit be known to all men. The Lord is near. Be anxious for nothing. (vv. 4–6a)

Paul exhorts us to *rejoice,* to *be patient,* and to *stop worrying*—easier said than done! But in verses 6b–7, he explains how it's possible.

But in everything by prayer and supplication with thanksgiving let your requests be made known to God. And the peace of God, which surpasses all comprehension, shall guard your hearts and your minds in Christ Jesus.

Isn't that good? When we pray, incomprehensible peace acts as a faithful watchdog over our hearts and minds. And anxiety is kept at bay when we talk things over with God.

We all know what it feels like to be a Martha. We need to dispel our anxious thoughts by focusing not on worry itself, but on God. So let's be willing to wait on God during tense times, when our strength sinks to low ebb, and commit ourselves to Christ and His resources instead of our own. And finally, let's unwrinkle our worried faces and radiate some joy and patience for a change—by praying!

 Living Insights

Worry. As if there isn't enough of it in our lives already, we are constantly having it imposed on us by TV shows and their advertisements. Gary Collins, in his book *Christian Counseling*, writes,

> [Worry] has been termed the "official emotion of our age," the basis of all neuroses, and "the most pervasive psychological phenomenon of our time."[4]

While the lesson is fresh in your mind, paraphrase the central idea behind each of the divine alternatives to worry.

A willingness to wait (Isa. 40:27–31): _____

_____

_____

_____

A commitment to Christ (Matt. 6:24–34): _____

_____

_____

_____

A priority of prayer (Phil. 4:4–7): _____

_____

_____

_____

---

4. Gary R. Collins, *Christian Counseling: A Comprehensive Guide* (Waco, Tex.: Word Books, 1980), p. 59.

"The Scriptures consistently expose people as both thirsty and foolish. We long for the satisfaction we were built to enjoy, but we all move away from God to find it."[5]

Which well do you find yourself dipping from most often to cool worry's blistering effects in your life?

Man-Made Wells	Divine Alternatives
Self-Reliance: "Try Harder"	A Willingness to Wait
Possessions: "Accumulate More"	A Commitment to Christ
Catharsis: "Tell More People"	A Priority of Prayer

Most of us know from experience that these man-made wells are dry; they don't possess the Living Water we thirst for. So let's put our buckets aside and begin right now to taste the difference of responding to worry God's way instead of our own. For the next few minutes do two things: (1) allow a specific worry to surface, and (2) identify its divine alternative and begin applying it!

Worry: _____

Divine alternative: _____

_____

---

5. Dr. Larry Crabb, from the study guide to *Inside Out* (Colorado Springs, Colo.: NavPress, 1988), p. 27.

Chapter 4

WHAT'S NECESSARY FOR VICTORY?

Romans 8:31–37; 1 Corinthians 9:24–27; 1 John 5:4, 7

S ometimes sermon titles create quite a stir—usually, the more sensational, the greater the interest.

One in particular brought people to church in droves. Back when television had just become popular, a certain pastor was having a hard time competing with prime-time viewing on Sunday nights, so he decided to do something about it. Weeks in advance, he announced the title of his upcoming Sunday evening message— "What the Bible Says about TV." On the night he gave it, the little church was buzzing. All the members were there, a few backsliders had come out of hiding, and even a couple of newspaper reporters were on the scene.

And they were all in for a big letdown.

The preacher strode to his pulpit, opened his Bible, and in stern tones declared, "I am now going to speak on what the Bible says about TV—Total Victory!"

Our lesson today has no titillating title or captivating caption. It just states the case. How can we have victory in the Christian life? What does having victory involve?

Many of us have misconceptions about what a victorious Christian life really is. Let's search the Scriptures to find out.

Five Things Victory Is Not

Romans 8 helps clear up some of our misunderstandings about victory.

> What then shall we say to these things? If God is for us, who is against us? He who did not spare His own Son, but delivered Him up for us all, how will He not also with Him freely give us all things? Who will bring a charge against God's elect? God is the one who justifies; who is the one who condemns? Christ Jesus is He who died, yes, rather who was raised, who is at the right hand of God, who also intercedes for us.

Who shall separate us from the love of Christ? Shall
tribulation, or distress, or persecution, or famine, or
nakedness, or peril, or sword? Just as it is written,
"For Thy sake we are being put to death
all day long,
We were considered as sheep to be
slaughtered."
But in all these things we overwhelmingly conquer
through Him who loved us. (vv. 31–37)

In a passage about victory, we would expect to find some military
imagery. Instead, we see an analogy of sheep waiting to be slaughtered. Just reading this passage helps us understand what victory is not.

Victory is not a once-for-all accomplishment.

Nowhere do we read that Christians can reach a plateau of
spirituality and remain there for the rest of their lives. Rather,
victory comes day by day.

Victory is not an emotional high.

Our walk has everything to do with our choices and little to do
with feelings. It's not the high you get on those starry nights by a
roaring campfire, with everyone singing "Kum Ba Yah." Or the exhilaration you feel when your dreams come true or your ship comes in.
Victory is possible despite our circumstances and despite our feelings.

Victory is not a dream reserved for supersaints.

Spiritual success does not depend on the number of years we
have known Christ or belonged to a church. It's available to any
Christian at any time.

Victory is not an independent achievement.

We achieve victory through Christ's death, Resurrection, and
intercession. Victory is unquestionably tied to Jesus—always.

*Victory is not something that happens to us as we passively
wait on the sidelines.*

The greatest enemy of Christian victory is passivity. Jesus' work
of redemption on the cross was active, and our striving for victory
is to be active as well.

Four Things Victory Includes

Let's look at 1 Corinthians 9 to discover what victory includes.
But before we do, we need to understand the background of the
passage.

27

Some of the Corinthians have challenged Paul's authority. So he raises some rhetorical questions to force them to consider his apostolic rights and privileges.

> Am I not free? Am I not an apostle? Have I not seen Jesus our Lord? Are you not my work in the Lord? If to others I am not an apostle, at least I am to you; for you are the seal of my apostleship in the Lord. (vv. 1–2)

Since the Corinthian believers have come into the Lord's family through Paul's faithful witness, he has the right to ask them for material support. Yet he has not done so.

> Or do only Barnabas and I not have a right to refrain from working? . . . If we sowed spiritual things in you, is it too much if we should reap material things from you? If others share the right over you, do we not more? Nevertheless, we did not use this right, but we endure all things, that we may cause no hindrance to the gospel of Christ. (vv. 6, 11–12)

Paul deliberately chooses to waive his rights for two reasons. The first reason is clear—so that non-Christians will recognize his clean motives and be won to Christ (vv. 12–23). The second is less obvious—it's for the sake of winning a personal victory. This reason is implied in verses 24–27, and it's these verses that give us the answer to what victory is made of.

Victory includes action.

This passage smells of sweat, panting, and agonizing work. It's full of athletic terms.

> Do you not know that those who run in a race all run, but only one receives the prize? Run in such a way that you may win. And everyone who competes in the games exercises self-control in all things. They then do it to receive a perishable wreath, but we an imperishable. Therefore I run in such a way, as not without aim; I box in such a way, as not beating the air; but I buffet my body and make it my slave, lest possibly, after I have preached to others, I myself should be disqualified. (vv. 24–27)

The word *compete* originates from the Greek word *agōnizomai,* which means "to agonize." Paul is probably thinking of the Isthmian games, which were much like our Olympics. The athletes involved took an oath, swearing they had given themselves to rigorous training for at least ten months and that they would not resort to trickery to win. Only appropriate training and compliance with the rules would yield victory and rewards.[1] It was active participants, not passive spectators, who won the prize.

Victory includes aim.

We can't take our eyes off the finish line; we can't lose sight of our goal. Look again at verse 26.

> I run in such a way, as not without aim; I box in such a way, as not beating the air.

We aren't to be like shadowboxers, striking at empty space. Our goals are to be clear because our enemy is real. To walk in victory means knowing where you're going and staying on track.

Victory includes discipline.

Discipline is just another word for self-control—the kind Paul talks about in verse 25.

> And everyone who competes in the games exercises self-control in all things.

Self-controlled people run with winning in mind. They train with consistency and sacrifice; they compete against their own tendency to ease up or give up; they keep an eye on the final tape; and they throw punches that hit the mark.

All of us in God's family have championship material down inside. The problem is, we have to overcome the spiritually flabby philosophy of our times. So often we opt for comfort and mediocrity, just basically yawning our way through life. We can turn that around if we decide to take hold of our lives.

> Press on. nothing in the world can take the place of persistence. Talent will not: nothing is more common than unsuccessful men with talent. Genius will not: unrewarded genius is almost a proverb. Education will not: the world is full of educated derelicts. Persistence and determination alone are overwhelmingly powerful.[2]

---

1. Merrill F. Unger, *Unger's Bible Dictionary,* 3d ed., rev. (Chicago, Ill.: Moody Press, 1966), pp. 389–90.

2. Calvin Coolidge, as quoted by Ted W. Engstrom in *Motivation to Last a Lifetime* (Grand Rapids, Mich.: Zondervan Publishing House, 1984), p. 76.

Victory takes persistence. It took twenty-two years for the McDonald's hamburger chain to make its first billion dollars. It took IBM forty-six years and Xerox sixty-three years to make their first billion.[3] If only we would apply that kind of determination to our walk with God! And part of that determination should be a wholesome fear of failure.

> Lest possibly, after I have preached to others, I myself should be disqualified. (v. 27b)

Disqualified? What a tragic thought. After having great information, insight, and truth, there is always the possibility of losing all reward—morally, spiritually, or personally. The fear of being disqualified should cause us to persist faithfully in our goals.

Victory includes reward.

All the winners in the Isthmian games received perishable rewards—money, education for their children, an olive or celery wreath for their heads. Our Olympians are given medals. But wreaths wilt and medals tarnish; only the Christian's rewards are imperishable.

> They then do it to receive a perishable wreath, but we an imperishable. (v. 25b)

We run toward a reward that will never rust or collect dust. But what does winning require of us?

Three Things Victory Requires

Spiritual victory has three prerequisites.

Victory requires spiritual birth.

The power that changed our status from enemies of God to children of God is the same power we need to overcome the world's allurements.

> For whatever is born of God overcomes the world. (1 John 5:4a)

Victory requires faith.

Victory depends on active trust—faith—in Christ's power. It is what we draw on each moment of the day.

> And this is the victory that has overcome the world— our faith. (v. 4b)

---

3. Denis Waitley, *Seeds of Greatness* (Old Tappan, N.J.: Fleming H. Revell, 1983), p. 200.

Victory requires truth.

The Spirit of God makes truth available to us, helping us know right from wrong, giving us direction.

And it is the Spirit who bears witness, because the Spirit is the truth. (v. 7)

When it comes to the Christian life, do you sometimes feel like you're more likely to receive a consolation prize than a winner's crown? Don't give up! Get off the couch, build up your muscles, and run!

 ## Living Insights

No one needs to remind a soldier going into battle, "Don't forget your rifle." Unfortunately, when it comes to spiritual combat, forgetting is exactly what Christians have a tendency to do—we forget our armor, our weapons, and even our reason for fighting the good fight. It must be a strange sight for God, looking down from His throne, to see so many Christians carelessly wandering onto the battlefield each day wearing only a dress, a suit, or blue jeans and a T-shirt.

The equipment we want to encourage you to check now is not your sword and shield, but rather your motivation for victory. Be transparent for a moment. Do you recognize yourself in any of the following statements?

Statement	Motivation
"I fight the good fight because deep down it's the praise and respect of my peers that keeps me going."	Acceptance from peers.
"I fight the good fight because when I don't, I feel guilty and don't sense God's love."	Performing to earn God's love.
"I fight the good fight because the Bible commands it. It doesn't matter what I like or dislike. The Bible says it, I do it, period."	Adhering to a rigid set of rules for acceptance.

All these have at least one thing in common: people searching for acceptance. But Romans 5 tells us that Christ has already made us acceptable to God. God accepts us not because of our works, but because of Christ's righteousness.

So let's follow Paul's example, who

> was constrained not by pressure to be acceptable but rather by the incomprehensible love of Christ (2 Cor. 5:14). *His root motivation was love.* He wanted to please God and serve men not to become acceptable but because he already was acceptable.[4] (emphasis added)

 *Living Insights*

Some of us cringe at the word *victory* since we're more painfully aware of our moments of weakness, doubt, and disillusionment than we are of any fleeting moments of triumph.

Slick solutions about "victorious living" that stem more from the American Dream than biblical reality are not what's needed. Instead, we need to enter the Christian's war room—the mind—and make some strategic plans to defeat the enemy on at least one front.

What major battle are you currently facing? A compromise in ethics . . . struggles with your mate . . . disappointment with God . . . some habitual sin? Describe the battle in the space provided.

My Battle

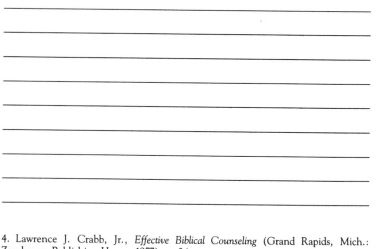

---

4. Lawrence J. Crabb, Jr., *Effective Biblical Counseling* (Grand Rapids, Mich.: Zondervan Publishing House, 1977), p. 24.

What principles from this chapter can you implement to gain victory? Do you need a change in perspective . . . in attitude . . . in action? Write out your course of action, being as specific as possible.

My Strategy

_____

_____

_____

_____

_____

_____

_____

_____

_____

Chapter 5

IS MY NEIGHBOR REALLY LOST?

Luke 10:25-37

Sometimes a return to basics is absolutely necessary.

When Vince Lombardi's Green Bay Packers were at their zenith, they were practically unbeatable. But they got overconfident and lost what should have been an easy game against the Chicago Bears on Soldier Field. Their coach was livid. When their plane landed in frozen-over Green Bay, he bused them directly to Lambeau Field, where they donned sweaty gear from the game. He began a nightlong practice session with the words: "Gentlemen, this is a football!"

How basic can you get? Can you imagine telling the Philadelphia Orchestra, "Ladies and gentlemen, this is a half note"? Or informing a librarian, "This is a book"? Can you picture saying, "Marine, this is a rifle" or "Mother of six, this is a diaper"?

When people begin to drift off track, it's time to return to the fundamentals—even in Christianity. What a football is to a team, what a half note is to a symphony, what a book is to a librarian, a neighbor is to a Christian. It's hypocritical to say we're interested in reaching the world for Christ if we're not concerned with reaching our own neighbors.

So let's get back to basics: "Christian, this is a neighbor!"

Who Is My Neighbor?

We can spend long hours, valuable energy, and millions of dollars working out strategies, initiating evangelistic crusades, establishing medical clinics and hospitals, building translation stations, and praying that governments will become and remain open to the gospel. Yet as wonderful as all of these efforts are, haven't we missed a basic ingredient? Outreach begins not overseas but closer to where we live—across the street, in our offices, in the shops we frequent.

But before we can begin to look at who our neighbors are, we must know who we are. Because who we are determines what we see, and what we see determines what we do.

Jesus knows this. Let's listen in on a conversation He's having with an attorney, recorded for us in Luke 10.

A Curious Question

The attorney begins the dialogue by asking a question:

"Teacher, what shall I do to inherit eternal life?" (v. 25)

And in good pedagogical manner, Jesus answers the man with another question.

And He said to him, "What is written in the Law? How does it read to you?" (v. 26)

Jewish lawyers in those days were experts in the Mosaic Law. They even wore a tiny leather pouch on the wrist or head, called a phylactery, which contained Old Testament verses. Jesus, knowing the purpose of phylacteries, has asked a question the man is sure to have the answer to, whether in the leather pouch or in his memory. And He was right. The attorney responds,

"You shall love the Lord your God with all your heart, and with all your soul, and with all your strength, and with all your mind; and your neighbor as yourself." (v. 27)

Jesus congratulates him for his right answer, but He also challenges the lawyer to go beyond Scripture memory and start putting his knowledge into action.

And He said to him, "You have answered correctly; do this, and you will live." (v. 28)

Today we would say, "That's it, plain and simple—now get at it!"

A Curious Twist

Lawyers like being on the offensive, but Jesus has just put this gentleman on the defensive, and he is reluctant to leave the scene bearing the burden of argument. So he shifts the burden back to Jesus and tries to squirm off the hook of responsibility by quibbling over the meaning of a word.

But wishing to justify himself, he said to Jesus, "And who is my neighbor?" (v. 29)

And Jesus capitalizes on the moment by telling a story that would explain His meaning beyond any doubt.

A Neighbor in Need

Jesus' story is about a man in need—a man who had taken a treacherous journey from Jerusalem to Jericho, where the way was craggy and steep and the altitude dropped thirty-six hundred feet over a distance of twenty miles. Robbers loved that lonely stretch of road. They could mug, assault, and rape without fear of intervention. It was a threatening and dangerous road for a person traveling alone.

> Jesus replied and said, "A certain man was going down from Jerusalem to Jericho; and he fell among robbers, and they stripped him and beat him, and went off leaving him half dead." (v. 30)

As Jesus continues, the drama heightens. What He says next will surely capture the lawyer's attention and draw him into a net of emotional identification.

> "And by chance a certain priest was going down on that road, and when he saw him, he passed by on the other side. And likewise a Levite also, when he came to the place and saw him, passed by on the other side." (vv. 31–32)

Two religious men sidestepped the wounded man. The first was a priest of Jerusalem's temple, a man whose profession was wrapped up in the things of God. The second was an assistant to the first, a Levite. Both men, religious professionals, saw the man but ignored the need.

Wilbur Rees, with biting sarcasm, could have written the following piece to these two myopic men.

> I would like to buy $3 worth of God, please, not enough to explode my soul or disturb my sleep, but just enough to equal a cup of warm milk or a snooze in the sunshine. I don't want enough of Him to make me love a black man or pick beets with a migrant. I want ecstasy, not transformation; I want the warmth of the womb, not a new birth. I want a pound of the Eternal in a paper sack. I would like to buy $3 worth of God, please.[1]

---

1. Wilbur Rees, as quoted in *When I Relax I Feel Guilty,* by Tim Hansel (Elgin, Ill.: David C. Cook Publishing Co., 1979), p. 49.

James says it a little more didactically.

> If a brother or sister is without clothing and in need of daily food, and one of you says to them, "Go in peace, be warmed and be filled," and yet you do not give them what is necessary for their body, what use is that? Even so faith, if it has no works, is dead, being by itself. (James 2:15–17)

Jesus goes on to contrast the response of the two religious men with that of another traveler—a man with unusual understanding and compassion.

> "But a certain Samaritan, who was on a journey, came upon him; and when he saw him, he felt compassion, and came to him, and bandaged up his wounds, pouring oil and wine on them; and he put him on his own beast, and brought him to an inn, and took care of him. And on the next day he took out two denarii and gave them to the innkeeper and said, 'Take care of him; and whatever more you spend, when I return, I will repay you.'" (Luke 10:33–35)

Samaritans were Jews who had intermarried with Assyrians and were despised by the full-blooded Jews. Devoted Jews going north would not defile themselves by traveling through Samaria. Instead, they would travel east, cross over the Jordan River into Perea, and completely bypass the despised country. And yet it was a Samaritan who showed compassion for a man who had already been turned down by Jerusalem's religious elite.

The Real Question: Am I a Merciful Neighbor?

The story Jesus has told is a parable that confronts the lawyer's prejudice and complacency—and perhaps ours as well. Let's listen to His concluding question and prepare to make our own personal response.

A Critical Question

Jesus brings His message home with a single question, thrust like a spear to its mark—the lawyer's heart.

> "Which of these three do you think proved to be a neighbor to the man who fell into the robbers' hands?" And he said, "The one who showed mercy toward him." And Jesus said to him, "Go and do the same." (vv. 36–37)

Jesus answers the lawyer's question from an unexpected angle. Instead of identifying who his neighbors are, Jesus shows him how to be a good neighbor himself. It's a message for us today as well. Jesus brings us into the realm of reality, where people hurt and cry and desire comfort. The real question we, along with the lawyer, must ask ourselves is this: Am *I* a good neighbor?

> We know love by this, that He laid down His life for us; and we ought to lay down our lives for the brethren. But whoever has the world's goods, and beholds his brother in need and closes his heart against him, how does the love of God abide in him? (1 John 3:16–17)

A Compassionate Plea

The lawyer's question, "Who is my neighbor?" is a good one, but it isn't the primary one. A much more basic question is, Who am I? Am I saved? If I am, do I risk reaching out to others?

The Samaritan, the priest, and the Levite all passed the same scene—a man stripped, beaten, and abandoned. But only one of them saw and responded to the need.

How about us? Do we see the needs of those around us and respond in compassion? Do we really see that if our neighbors are without Christ, they are lost and in as bad of shape as the man on the road to Jericho?

Stripped. The people we meet who don't know the Savior are stripped. They are stripped of the righteousness of Christ, of hope when they stand before the throne of judgment, of any possibility of escape from hell.

Beaten. The unsaved are beaten by a world that's overwhelming, by a system that is daily ripping them off, by a web of lies that promises peace but gives them pressure and heartache instead.

Abandoned. The enemy that stripped and beat them now leaves them with nothing—no hope, no future, nothing but the fleeting delight of the present moment.

Reaching the world for Christ doesn't begin in some foreign land, but right here within our own hearts. We must know whether we ourselves are saved and whether we're willing to act on Christ's command for compassion. Then we will not need to ask who our neighbors are—we will see them everywhere. And our hearts will tell us what to do.

According to Plato, Socrates once said that the unexamined life is not worth living. It might also be said that the unexamined faith is not worth believing.

Instead of allowing the lawyer to put Him on trial, Jesus turned the tables and drew him into a greatly needed self-examination through the use of a parable (Luke 10:30–37).

For the next few moments, step up to the witness stand and allow the following Scriptures to examine you and your understanding of the question, Am I a Christian?

Look up the following verses; then answer the corresponding questions.

Romans 3:23. Do I see myself as being willfully disobedient to God?

_____

Romans 6:23a. Do I believe there will be a consequence to my sin?

_____

Ephesians 2:8–9. What good works can I do to save myself?

_____

_____

Romans 5:8–9. How did God demonstrate His love for me?

_____

_____

John 11:25. Do I realize the difference between intellectually knowing *about* Christ and personally trusting in Him?

_____

_____

_____

Many think acting like a Christian is the way to become one. But God has declared that there is only one way of becoming a Christian, and that is through faith in Jesus Christ alone.

How do you plea?

Someone has said that a good indication of our closeness to Christ is the degree of our compassion.

As we encounter others on the road of life, are we like the Pharisee, saying, "God, I thank Thee that I am not like other people: swindlers, unjust, adulterers . . ." (Luke 18:11)?

Or are we reminded of the familiar words, There but for the grace of God go I, and moved to show the compassion we have been given from Christ?

Pray and meditate for a moment, asking God to open your eyes to at least one "neighbor" whom you might be callously stepping over in your daily pursuits. Write down that person's name:

_____.

Next, brainstorm some concrete ways you might demonstrate the love of Christ to this person.

_____

_____

_____

_____

_____

_____

_____

_____

_____

_____

_____

_____

_____

_____

_____

_____

Chapter 6

WHAT MAKES A REBEL RETURN?

Selected Scripture

Jubilee magazine carried an attention-grabbing story in its April 1984 issue. It was about a woman whose church had disciplined her for sexual immorality—but the whole thing had backfired. She didn't deny the affair, but, according to the church elders, she refused to repent, so she was expelled from the fellowship. Outraged by the invasion of her privacy, she took the congregation to court—and won!

This article brings a prickly question to the forefront—the question of repentance. In our lesson today, let's unravel this knotty issue and see how Scripture addresses it.

An Issue in Need of Consideration

Why is it that some people kneel in humility when confronted with wrong, while others dig in their heels and resist? The woman in the article openly admitted to having an affair. She just resented being called to task over it.

Let's bring the issue closer to home. Suppose that sinning person was your friend, or even your spouse? What would you do if there was a refusal to repent? Conversely, how would you respond if this person wanted to restore the relationship?

Tough questions. What does cause a rebellious person to return to truth? Not just halfhearted repentance, enough to salve the conscience and sneak back in the door, but wholehearted remorse. The question "What makes a rebel return?" is a hard one. So let's take a hard look at the Scriptures for an answer.

Some Scriptures Worth Our Attention

This business of rebellion is nothing new. The questions that perplex us have been puzzling people since Isaiah's time, and even before. Take a look at Isaiah 31:6.

> Return to Him from whom you have deeply defected,
> O sons of Israel.

Isaiah is addressing the Israelites, who have strayed from the side of God. And not just a few steps off the path—this is determined, willful disobedience, a deep defection.[1] Isaiah's rebuke isn't complicated. It's a simple solution to a deep-rooted problem, very much like his impassioned plea in chapter 55.

> Seek the Lord while He may be found;
> Call upon Him while He is near.
> Let the wicked forsake his way,
> And the unrighteous man his thoughts;
> And let him return to the Lord,
> And He will have compassion on him;
> And to our God,
> For He will abundantly pardon. (vv. 6–7)

The New Testament also addresses the issue of sin and restoration. First Corinthians 5 offers an example in the story of a scandalous event and Paul's response to the way the church had handled it. Centuries ago one of our modern-day problems was discovered in ancient Corinth—incest. And it surfaced in the church (v. 1)! The church's response was astonishing. Instead of confronting the offenders, they expressed understanding and grace . . . and let it continue. Paul was outraged.

> For I, on my part, though absent in body but present in spirit, have already judged him who has so committed this, as though I were present. . . . I have decided to deliver such a one to Satan for the destruction of his flesh, that his spirit may be saved in the day of the Lord Jesus. . . . I wrote to you not to associate with any so-called brother if he should be an immoral person, or covetous, or an idolater, or a reviler, or a drunkard, or a swindler—not even to eat with such a one. . . . Remove the wicked man from among yourselves. (vv. 3, 5, 11, 13b)

Some of the most severe words in Scripture. The Corinthians were quick to remedy their mistake, but then they went to the other extreme—the sinner repented, and they wouldn't let him back in

---

1. Some people protest that a Christian who falls deeply into sin wasn't really a Christian to begin with. But the way God dealt with rebellious Israel would contradict this line of thinking. In Isaiah 44:21b–22 God said to Israel, "*I have formed you, you are My servant,* / O Israel, you will not be forgotten by Me. / I have wiped out your transgressions like a thick cloud, / And your sins like a heavy mist. / Return to Me, for I have redeemed you" (emphasis added). Our standing with God isn't based on the depth of our sin, but on our relationship to Him.

their fellowship. Like some of today's Christians, they underreacted when it came to sin and overreacted when it came to punishment. In 2 Corinthians 2:6–8 Paul brings them back into balance.

Sufficient for such a one is this punishment which was inflicted by the majority, so that on the contrary you should rather forgive and comfort him, lest somehow such a one be overwhelmed by excessive sorrow. Wherefore I urge you to reaffirm your love for him.

Other New Testament passages deal with similar topics. In Galatians 6:1 we learn how to restore sinners, while James 5:19–20 describes the good one does in confronting. Second Thessalonians 3:6–15 details the type of action to be taken with a sinning believer, and Hebrews 12:5–13 deals with the discipline of God in the lives of His children. All these passages leave us with several main thoughts. First: defecting or wandering does occur . . . and God never takes it lightly. Second: when there is disobedience, the need is for repentance and restoration . . . and God uses various ways to bring that about. Third: when the rebel returns, there needs to be forgiveness, pardon, and affirmation.

An Analysis of Four Changed Lives

Woven through Scripture are the stories of many lives that have been changed by a penitent spirit, and each one shows various means that God uses to cause the rebel to come home.

David

You've met him before—the shepherd turned king, the sweet singer of Israel whose song turned sour. One of the darkest periods of his life was when he seduced Bathsheba and murdered her husband. Instead of admitting his sin and confessing it to God, David attempted to hide it, adding lies and hypocrisy to his list of sins. He may have managed to fool some of his people, but he couldn't escape the all-seeing eyes of God.

But the thing that David had done was evil in the sight of the Lord. (2 Sam. 11:27b)

So what did God do with His rebellious, adulterous, hypocritical servant? He dispatched someone to confront him.

Then the Lord sent Nathan to David. (12:1)

You know the rest. Nathan told David a story of a rich man who took a poor man's only lamb to feed his guest so he wouldn't have to kill one of his own. David indignantly declared that the man

43

deserved to die. With penetrating, uncompromising words, the prophet pointed his finger in the face of the king and uttered those unforgettable words—"You are the man!" (v. 7). Hearing those words, David crumbled and returned to God.

But God does not always use a confronting prophet, as we will see in the case of David's son.

Solomon

This son, like David's other sons, spent much of his life away from the Lord. In fact, his whole lifestyle had been one of trying to drain from the world all it had to offer. He reveled in wine, women, and song; he built buildings and took trips; he did anything and everything, and money was no object. Yet at the end of his journal he wrote,

"Vanity of vanities, . . . all is vanity!" (Eccles. 12:8)

Repentance for Solomon didn't come in the face of an accusing prophet but in the face of utter emptiness. The words of his return hold an admonition for his readers.

Remember also your Creator in the days of your youth, before the evil days come and the years draw near when you will say, "I have no delight in them"; . . . The conclusion, when all has been heard, is: fear God and keep His commandments, because this applies to every person. For God will bring every act to judgment, everything which is hidden, whether it is good or evil. (12:1, 13–14)

Do you know someone like Solomon, a friend or a child or a mate, who is wallowing in the world system? Have you been waiting for rebellion to run its course, since no amount of confrontation has made an impact? Don't stop waiting. And don't stop praying. By God's grace, the day may come when sin's sparkle will tarnish and all that so-called freedom will be seen as the worst kind of bondage.

With some people, God uses confrontation or desolation to bring them back to Him. But sometimes, He must use a tragedy, as He did with Jonah.

Jonah

Clearly and undeniably, God had spoken to Jonah. He hadn't stuttered or hesitated or been oblique in His command. He had said simply and clearly, "Go to Nineveh" (Jon. 1:2). Remember what happened? God's prophet became a fugitive . . . a rebel on the run.

> But Jonah rose up to flee to Tarshish from the presence of the Lord. (v. 3a)

It was an act of wild disobedience—Jonah hoped to run away from Jehovah by sailing to Tarshish (vv. 3b, 10). There was no Nathan to confront him, and he wasn't in despair over the emptiness of life. Verse 5 tells us he was sleeping like a baby, even while the ship was in danger of sinking.

But God wasn't sleeping.

> And the Lord hurled a great wind on the sea and there was a great storm on the sea so that the ship was about to break up. . . . [And] they said to [Jonah], "What should we do to you that the sea may become calm for us?"—for the sea was becoming increasingly stormy. And he said to them, "Pick me up and throw me into the sea. Then the sea will become calm for you. . . ." So they picked up Jonah, threw him into the sea, and the sea stopped its raging. . . . And the Lord appointed a great fish to swallow Jonah, and Jonah was in the stomach of the fish three days and three nights. (vv. 4, 11–12a, 15, 17)

It was a God-appointed calamity. God doesn't always use a confronting prophet or the sheer boredom of the world system. Sometimes he brings on a tragedy. And in this instance, it certainly brought about the desired effect. By the time God released Jonah from the fish, His purpose had been accomplished.

> Now the word of the Lord came to Jonah the second time, saying, "Arise, go to Nineveh. . . ." So Jonah arose and went to Nineveh. (3:1–3a)

God will not be outdone or outrun.

The Prodigal Son

Most of us are familiar with the story of the prodigal son found in Luke 15. Let's pick up the story when the pockets of the prodigal son are turned inside out.

> "Now when he had spent everything, a severe famine occurred in that country, and he began to be in need. And he went and attached himself to one of the citizens of that country, and he sent him into his fields to feed swine. And he was longing to fill his stomach with the pods that the swine were eating, and no one was giving anything to him. But when he came to his

45

senses, he said, 'How many of my father's hired men have more than enough bread, but I am dying here with hunger! I will get up and go to my father, and will say to him, "Father, I have sinned against heaven, and in your sight; I am no longer worthy to be called your son; make me as one of your hired men." ' And he got up and came to his father. But while he was still a long way off, his father saw him, and felt compassion for him, and ran and embraced him, and kissed him." (vv. 14–20)

What drew the boy back? A confronting prophet? No. The boredom and emptiness of it all? Well, not exactly. A tragedy or calamity? Not really. It was the love and acceptance of a home and a family. Once the boy came to his senses, he was drawn back to his home—and to his father. And that loving, accepting dad embraced his son.

Summary and Observations

Sometimes it takes a Nathan to say "You're wrong!" Other times, dissatisfaction with the sheer boredom and emptiness of the world pushes people back to God. Although we dread it, sometimes God uses calamity. Still other times, the love and acceptance of home turn them around.

But although the methods may vary, there are some things about God that never change.

First: *He is a jealous Groom.* When His bride flirts with the world and embraces sin, He never yawns and looks the other way.

Second: *He is a sovereign Lord.* When His servants rebel and run, He pursues.

Third: *He is a compassionate Father.* When His children come back, He forgives, accepts, and affirms them.

Living Insights   STUDY ONE

There's nothing easy about true repentance. Voluntarily bringing up our own sins is like uncovering a wound and asking someone to touch it.

But could it be that God is trying to get your attention through one of the means we discussed in our lesson? Take another look at each of the four people we studied and answer the questions that pertain to you.

David

King David sits tensed upon his throne with the wearied, desperate look of a fox about to run out of places to hide. Once again, his conscience is hounding him over what had started with his affair with Bathsheba. But again, David's guilt tries to hide behind the familiar, tangled undergrowth of rationalization.

> Conscience: You shall not covet your neighbor's wife.
> Guilt: It's no big deal. Just bring me that woman I saw bathing.
>
> Conscience: You shall not bear false witness against your neighbor.
> Guilt: It's no big deal. Just bring me her husband. He'll think it's his own baby.
>
> Conscience: You shall not murder.
> Guilt: It's no big deal. Just pull away from him in battle so he'll be killed.

David pulls himself away from the tiresome debate, his eyes adjusting to the morning light that streams into his palace and illuminates the figure of the day's first petitioner.

"Oh . . . hello, Nathan."

- Have you become so calloused by your sin that God has had to place a Nathan in your path? How will you respond?

Solomon

It's the middle of the day, and Solomon has come in to lie down. His servants hear the sighs that he is not even aware of. Lying lifelessly still, only his eyes move. He is looking for something. Solomon's mind searches among his many pursuits for the hope and purpose he does not feel. Rest evades him, and his search produces only the stale ache of emptiness, futility. The guards hear another sigh.

- Is God speaking to you through the emptiness sin has brought into your life? Where will you look to find meaning?

_____

_____

_____

Jonah

The prophet has sown willful disobedience and he's now reaping a harvest of calamity—the kind that makes him despair even of life. There is no place to hide, no shelter, no protection or quiet respite. Jonah's circumstances come upon him like a flash flood, uprooting him like a tree caught in the swift current. Desperately, he builds a raft of repentance before the undertow of his own sins pulls him beneath the surface to drown.

- Are you facing tragedy in your life now? Not all tragedy is a result of personal sin, but are you suffering like Jonah because of clear rebellion against God in some area?

_____

_____

_____

The Prodigal Son

"Here, pigs," barely escapes in a choked whisper as he feels his throat tightening. Through his tears he finally realizes he's hit bottom. He wishes it were all only a bad dream, but the raw smell of the pigsty clears his mind of any illusions. He feels like screaming, "What am I doing here?" He has never felt so alone.

It is only a little while later that the pigs eat the empty slop basket—dropped by the hungry boy who has remembered he is a son and has set off for home to find his father.

- Is there someone in your life who is drawing you toward repentance?

_____

_____

_____

Most of us would probably want God to use us as a means of leading someone to repentance. But do we realize the cost of that desire? It wouldn't be easy.

It would mean not looking the other way, practicing patience, enduring hurt.

It would mean continued prayer, confronting out of love instead of irritation, wanting to understand instead of reprimand.

It might mean grieving, risking rejection, examining our own lives.

Sound involved?

> "Greater love has no one than this, that one lay down
> his life for his friends." (John 15:13)

Spend some time studying the following references, and answer the question, "Is there someone for whom God could use me as a means to encourage repentance?"

Galatians 6:1	1 Thessalonians 5:14–15
Matthew 18:15–17	Ephesians 4:29
2 Thessalonians 3:6–15	Proverbs 25:11–12; 27:5–6, 17

Chapter 7

CAN "ORDINARY PEOPLE" MAKE A CONTRIBUTION?

Acts 8–9

O ne of the archenemies of evangelism is false propaganda—
wrong ideas that get embedded in the Christian's mind before
the truth can find lodging.

The propaganda carries a line something like this: "Service is for
superstars—spiritual giants like the apostle Paul, Hudson Taylor,
George Müller, Jim Elliot. It's not for ordinary people like me." It's
almost as if a sinister force creeps into every church nursery and
whispers, "Psst, hey kid, wake up! Being a missionary is for superstars
and you don't qualify. Now go back to sleep." So, many of us grow
up believing that serving God is for somebody else.

Regarding Giants, Celebrities, and Superstars

But if we take a closer look at the superstars of ministry, we find
that they struggle with the same things we do: doubt, temptation,
greed, self-pity, prayerlessness, selfishness. Warren Wiersbe, in his
book *Walking with the Giants*, looks at some great men of the past—
like Spurgeon, Tozer, G. Campbell Morgan—and reminds us of their
earthiness as he presents some "up close and personal" glimpses into
their lives. One well-known person exhibited a perfectionist nature.
Many were given to depression and fear of failure, while one man
was confined to his bed.[1] They were all ordinary people—but that's
difficult for us to accept. How easy it is to forget Paul's reminder in
1 Corinthians 1!

> For consider your calling, brethren, that there were
> not many wise according to the flesh, not many
> mighty, not many noble; but God has chosen the
> foolish things of the world to shame the wise, and God
> has chosen the weak things of the world to shame the
> things which are strong, and the base things of the
> world and the despised, God has chosen, the things
> that are not, that He might nullify the things that are,
> that no man should boast before God. (vv. 26–29)

1. See Warren Wiersbe's *Walking with the Giants* (Grand Rapids, Mich.: Baker Book
House, 1976).

The traditional missionary ad campaign sends a message that intimidates us rather than motivates us. And yet God's plan for evangelism rests with ordinary people.

> But we have this treasure in earthen vessels, that the surpassing greatness of the power may be of God and not from ourselves. (2 Cor. 4:7)

Someone has paraphrased this verse, "We have this treasure in a peanut butter jar." The wealth of the gospel is contained in run-of-the-mill human beings. A story about Oliver Cromwell illustrates what God wants us to do with that wealth.

At the time, England was running out of silver for making coins. So Cromwell sent his men to the cathedrals to see if they could find any silver there. They reported, "The only silver we could find is in the statues of the saints standing in the corners"—to which the crusty statesman replied, "Good! We'll melt down the saints and put them into circulation!"[2]

That's where all saints belong—in circulation! We don't belong in the corner of some church building, gathering dust. We belong out among people.

Ordinary People Doing Unlikely Things

Let's look at a few ordinary people in Acts 8 and 9 who did some unlikely things because they were available to God. These people are not the most obvious ones in Scripture, or even in these passages. But they are significant because they found ways to get into circulation.

Acts 8:1–2

This passage opens on the scene following Stephen's stoning (7:54–60). The apostle Paul had not yet been converted; he was still known as Saul. In full agreement with the stoning, he even held the robes of the witnesses during the execution. It would be easy to focus on him as the prominent character in this drama, but as we read verse 1 of chapter 8, let's pay attention to the other people involved.

> And Saul was in hearty agreement with putting him to death. And on that day a great persecution arose against the church in Jerusalem; and they were all scattered throughout the regions of Judea and Samaria, except the apostles.

2. As quoted by Charles R. Swindoll, in Encourage Me (Portland, Oreg.: Multnomah Press, 1982), p. 61.

The Jerusalem Christians had been enjoying close fellowship under the guidance of the apostles, but that came to an abrupt end. God was melting them down and putting them into circulation. Before they left, however, they took time to do one important thing.

> And some devout men buried Stephen, and made loud lamentation over him. (v. 2)

Can you imagine conducting a funeral service for a friend? These men did not hesitate, even though the fires of persecution were being fanned by an overzealous Pharisee.

> Saul began ravaging the church, entering house after house; and dragging off men and women, he would put them in prison. (v. 3)

Danger was ablaze in the church. Paul reminds us in Acts 26 of his actions during that time: he threw Christians into prison, cast his vote for their death sentences, tried to force them to blaspheme, hunted them down in synagogues, and even pursued them to foreign cities (vv. 10–11). It's a lesson for us today—embrace the ministry, and even such a simple act as a burial may open up an onslaught of personal suffering.

Acts 8:4

When Saul's rock of persecution hit the lake, it sent ripples of evangelism in every direction. Instead of stopping Christianity, he spread it! And through ordinary people.

> Therefore, those who had been scattered went about preaching the word. (v. 4)

The phrase "went about preaching the word" is commonly used in Acts to describe missionary activity. The simplicity of the phrase paints a great picture of the methods they used—nothing fancy, nothing planned. They just did it, wherever they were. Michael Green adds an insightful comment:

> The very fact that we are so imperfectly aware of how evangelism was carried out and by whom, should make us sensitive to the possibility that the little man, the unknown ordinary man, the man who left no literary remains was the prime agent in mission.[3]

---

3. Michael Green, *Evangelism in the Early Church* (Grand Rapids, Mich.: William B. Eerdmans Publishing Co., 1970), p. 172.

A man named Philip[4] was one of those prime agents.

> And Philip went down to the city of Samaria and began proclaiming Christ to them. And the multitudes with one accord were giving attention to what was said by Philip, as they heard and saw the signs which he was performing. For in the case of many who had unclean spirits, they were coming out of them shouting with a loud voice; and many who had been paralyzed and lame were healed. And there was much rejoicing in that city. (vv. 5–8)

Philip and the others who preached were unlikely missionary candidates—they weren't professionals; they had no seminary training. But they had Jesus, and that was enough. At its inception, Christianity was a movement of ordinary people whose hearts were on fire with the conviction that Jesus was worth talking about—even though their lives could have been extinguished for it.

Acts 9:10–20

Ananias of Damascus was another common person who was used greatly by God. We normally spend our time on the first nine verses of Acts 9—the story of Paul's conversion. But the verses that follow have a story to tell too.

> Now there was a certain disciple at Damascus, named Ananias; and the Lord said to him in a vision, "Ananias." And he said, "Behold, here am I, Lord." And the Lord said to him, "Arise and go to the street called Straight, and inquire at the house of Judas for a man from Tarsus named Saul, for behold, he is praying, and he has seen in a vision a man named Ananias come in and lay his hands on him, so that he might regain his sight." (vv. 10–12)

This was like getting an order to start a Bible study with Christianity's public enemy number one.

> But Ananias answered, "Lord, I have heard from many about this man, how much harm he did to Thy saints at Jerusalem; and here he has authority from the chief priests to bind all who call upon Thy name." (vv. 13–14)

---

4. The Philip mentioned here should not be confused with the Philip who was one of Jesus' original twelve disciples. "The Early Church added 'the apostle' to distinguish him from Philip the evangelist and deacon [spoken of in Acts 6.5]." *The Zondervan Pictorial Encyclopedia of the Bible*, gen. ed. Merrill C. Tenney (Grand Rapids, Mich.: Zondervan Publishing House, 1976), vol. 4, p. 758.

Saul's notorious reputation would intimidate anybody. But God's next words put an end to Ananias' reluctance.

> But the Lord said to him, "Go, for he is a chosen instrument of Mine, to bear My name before the Gentiles and kings and the sons of Israel; for I will show him how much he must suffer for My name's sake." (vv. 15–16)

So Ananias went to the street called Straight, looked up Judas' house, and began to minister to Saul.

> "Brother Saul, the Lord Jesus, who appeared to you on the road by which you were coming, has sent me so that you may regain your sight, and be filled with the Holy Spirit." And immediately there fell from his eyes something like scales, and he regained his sight, and he arose and was baptized; and he took food and was strengthened. Now for several days he was with the disciples who were at Damascus. (vv. 17b–19)

Ananias was privileged to confirm Saul as the Lord's own child. But more importantly, he discipled and encouraged him—an ordinary man instructing a gifted individual.

Acts 9:21–25

Saul began to work as intensely for Christ as he had against Him. But his radical change upset the opposition, and they decided to kill him (vv. 20–24). Their plans were thwarted, however, because some ordinary men helped Saul escape.

> But his disciples took him by night, and let him down through an opening in the wall, lowering him in a large basket. (v. 25)

We aren't told who held the ropes, but Paul never forgot these brave friends. In his letter to the Corinthians, as he recounted his sufferings for Christ, he gave this event a mention of special significance (2 Cor. 11:32–33).

Acts 9:26–28

After his escape, Saul went to Jerusalem. There he met another ordinary man who would play a major role in his life.

> And when he had come to Jerusalem, he was trying to associate with the disciples; and they were all afraid of him, not believing that he was a disciple. But

> Barnabas took hold of him and brought him to the
> apostles and described to them how he had seen the
> Lord on the road, and that He had talked to him, and
> how at Damascus he had spoken out boldly in the
> name of Jesus. (vv. 26–27)

The apostles embraced Saul because Barnabas vouched for him.
And the acceptance Saul received from these men gave wings to
the message of the Cross.

> And he was with them moving about freely in Jeru-
> salem, speaking out boldly in the name of the Lord.
> (v. 28)

Barnabas helped Paul become established in the ministry. He
gave Paul encouragement and support, not only in this instance but
throughout their association together (see also 11:22–26), promot-
ing Paul's abilities selflessly. He was content to be a scene-shifter on
Paul's brilliant stage.

Ordinary people are wonderful. They do extraordinary things,
like bury a friend, talk to someone about Christ, disciple important
people, help a special person get started in a successful ministry. If
you think of yourself as a plain, ordinary person, without superstar
qualities, take heart. There are no little people in God's economy.

🐚 Living Insights

Most of us have prayed for the salvation of someone who is close
to our heart. But have you ever stopped to consider *how* that's going
to happen?

Maybe a tract left anonymously on the door . . . slogans on
bumper stickers or T-shirts . . . Christian graffiti on water towers
and bridges? Perhaps toothbrushes with Scriptures printed on them,
or a ploy for an evangelistic rally cleverly disguised as an innocent
dinner invitation.

As you try to picture these things having a meaningful impact
on this person, you realize something seems wrong. Something is
missing in the methods. But what?

The warm, real contact of ordinary people.

Even God didn't just open the back door of heaven and holler
out that He loved us. Instead, He demonstrated His love by becoming one of us, by getting down on our level through the flesh and

blood of His Son (Rom. 5:8). Christ's life, death, and Resurrection provide us with the tangible proof of His love that we all long for.

But who will demonstrate to my brother Christ's sacrificial love? Who will demonstrate to my sister Christ's tears over sin and death? Who will demonstrate to my father or mother Christ's willingness to heal bitterness?

Is there anyone who will take the time to *show* Christ and not just *tell?*

Ordinary people can. Will you?

- Has God placed a lost person in your life—perhaps someone who lives or works beside you? Write down that person's name, and think of some concrete ways of *showing* that person Christ's love.

_____

_____

_____

_____

_____

_____

_____

_____

_____

_____

_____

_____

_____

Many of us have felt like George Bailey, the main character in the film classic *It's a Wonderful Life.* George has grand visions for his life that always get thwarted somehow, leaving him feeling chained to a very ordinary life in his little hometown of Bedford Falls.

Like George, many of us tend to label our lives and activities as "important" or "ordinary," "spiritual" or "secular."

Take a moment to list some of the things you usually put into each category.

Spiritual or Important	Secular or Ordinary
Reading my Bible	*Grocery shopping*

Is this kind of categorizing what the Scriptures teach? Or have we bought into what Franky Schaeffer describes as "a strange truncated unscriptural view of spirituality . . . something separate from the rest of real life"? He goes on to say that the spiritual life sometimes seems "above ordinary things; it [is] cut off and not part of the everyday working out of our lives. . . . Thus, certain things increasingly [are] regarded as spiritual and other things as secular."[5]

Continued on next page

5. Franky Schaeffer, *Addicted to Mediocrity* (Westchester, Ill.: Good News Publishers, Crossway Books, 1981), p. 27.

Take a moment to look up the following verses and see how God views the things we consider ordinary and unimportant. Write down what you find.

- Romans 12:1 (our bodies): _____

  _____

- 2 Corinthians 10:5 (our thoughts): _____

  _____

- Philippians 2:3–5 (our attitudes): _____

  _____

- Colossians 3:23 (our work): _____

  _____

- Matthew 22:37 (our total selves): _____

  _____

Finally, in exasperation over his life, George wishes he'd never been born. His wish is granted, and through a frightening barrage of discoveries, George sees how significant his "ordinary" life has actually been. As C. S. Lewis wrote in *The Weight of Glory*,

> There are no *ordinary* people. You have never talked to a mere mortal. Nations, cultures, arts, civilization —these are mortal, and their life is to ours as the life of a gnat. But it is immortals whom we joke with, work with, marry, snub, and exploit—immortal horrors or everlasting splendours.[6]

6. C. S. Lewis, *The Weight of Glory* (Grand Rapids, Mich.: William B. Eerdmans Publishing Co., 1949), p. 15.

Chapter 8

WILL YOU LEAD OR LAG?

1 Corinthians 14:33, Exodus 18

T he ministry of a local church is like an iceberg—not because it's cold and clumsy, but because much of what goes on is beneath the surface and away from public awareness. As an iceberg reveals only an eighth to a tenth of its mass above the water, so the visible leadership of a church is only a small portion of its ministry.

Think about your own church—the teachers; the small-group leaders; the greeters; those who help with children, teen, or adult ministries; the various officers and special task groups. These volunteers are the secret of a ministry's future.

Have you thought of becoming one of those volunteers? Or are you involved in selecting people to serve? Either way, it's important to look at leadership from God's point of view.

A Statement of What Pleases God

First Corinthians 14 is Paul's attempt to correct the disorder and confusion that was present in the first-century church at Corinth. Although we won't be studying that church's problems in this lesson, we can learn some important information about God from Paul's words in verse 33.

Negatively: God is not pleased with confusion.

The beginning of this verse gives us our first clue to God's character.

For God is not a God of confusion. (v. 33a)

The word *confusion* means "disorder" or "unrest." It may also be described as a "disruption of the peace of the community . . . by orgiastic impulses in the gatherings of the congregation."[1] In other words, unrestrained emotions. God does not find pleasure in congregational meetings where feelings run rampant and confusion abounds.

---

1. Gerhard Kittel, ed., *Theological Dictionary of the New Testament* (Grand Rapids, Mich.: William B. Eerdmans Publishing Co., 1965), vol. 3, p. 446.

Positively: God is pleased with order.

The last part of verse 33 tells us what God does prefer.

> But [God is a God] of peace, as in all the churches of
> the saints.

The context surrounding this verse shows us that God is pleased when things are done in a well-organized manner. He's pleased with a church that is well-managed, with a body of believers who exhibit self-control. God loves things that are well-ordered. Do you doubt that? Then spend a few hours with a microscope or a telescope observing the Creator's organization of the universe.

Principles for Good Leadership

Moses is one of the most visible leaders in the Old Testament. In fact, several books trace his career: Exodus, Leviticus, Numbers, and Deuteronomy; and an entire chapter in Exodus is devoted to the subject of his leadership style. In this chapter, we see Moses' need for organization and how God uses a wise man to teach him some important principles for good leadership.

An Evaluation

In the first eleven verses of Exodus 18, we see Jethro, Moses' father-in-law, coming to visit the Israelites' camp. When he arrives, he and Moses cordially exchange greetings, bowing and kissing and catching up on news. It's a moment of warmth and family contact, and Jethro gives God praise for what He has done through his son-in-law.

> So Jethro said, "Blessed be the Lord who delivered you
> from the hand of the Egyptians and from the hand of
> Pharaoh, and who delivered the people from under the
> hand of the Egyptians. Now I know that the Lord is
> greater than all the gods; indeed, it was proven when
> they dealt proudly against the people." (vv. 10–11)

But the next day, Moses gets back to work, and Jethro sits back to observe.

> And it came about the next day that Moses sat to
> judge the people, and the people stood about Moses
> from the morning until the evening. (v. 13)

Jethro frowns with displeasure when he sees Moses attempting to meet the needs of too many people by himself. And he lets Moses know how he feels.

Now when Moses' father-in-law saw all that he was doing for the people, he said, "What is this thing that you are doing for the people? Why do you alone sit as judge and all the people stand about you from morning until evening?" (v. 14)

Perhaps you feel a little like Moses. Maybe you keep adding things to your schedule that threaten to pull you under. If so, the following counsel from Jethro may help keep your head above water.

Some Suggestions

One person, no matter how gifted, cannot do a big job all alone. A gifted person can do a lot, but no person is gifted enough to run a ministry alone.

And Moses' father-in-law said to him, "The thing that you are doing is not good. You will surely wear out, both yourself and these people who are with you, for the task is too heavy for you; you cannot do it alone." (vv. 17–18)

It may appear very spiritual to be overworked, but remember: God is pleased when things are done in a well-ordered way—in a way that brings exhilaration, not exhaustion.

High-visibility leadership is still needed, but that role must be limited. Jethro knows the problem is serious enough that he needs to say something to Moses.

"Now listen to me: I shall give you counsel, and God be with you. You be the people's representative before God, and you bring the disputes to God, then teach them the statutes and the laws, and make known to them the way in which they are to walk, and the work they are to do." (vv. 19–20)

Jethro's counsel sounds like it came straight from one of today's management seminars. But long before Harvard business school heard of it, God spoke it through a Midianite priest.

Big loads must be borne by many, and the helpers must be selected carefully. Jethro has two things in mind as he gives Moses his advice—the work has to get done, and the leader needs relief.

"Furthermore, you shall select out of all the people able men who fear God, men of truth, those who hate dishonest gain; and you shall place these over them, as leaders of thousands, of hundreds, of fifties and of tens. And let them judge the people at all times; and let it be that every major dispute they will bring to you, but every minor dispute they themselves will judge. So it will be easier for you, and they will bear the burden with you." (vv. 21–22)

Where did we get the idea that Maalox, Alka-Seltzer, and Excedrin are the executive symbols of spiritual success? Who led us to believe that working in God's vineyard should be backbreaking labor, without a moment's leisure? If doing God's work becomes a burden, then the load needs to be properly distributed.

But not to just anybody. Jethro specifies that these people must be "able," or skilled for the task. They must also fear God and have integrity—be people who will refuse to compromise when decisions need to be made. And finally, they must "hate dishonest gain." Their focus cannot be on money.

The result of work delegated to qualified helpers is a peaceful, organized ministry that is pleasing to God.

"If you do this thing and God so commands you, then you will be able to endure, and all these people also will go to their place in peace." (v. 23)

When there is proper management, two things happen: leaders don't wear out and harmony prevails. When leaders are burned out or there is discord, it's a sign of poor management.

Needed Changes

To Moses' credit, he didn't try to justify his management style or get defensive about it. Instead, he admitted that it needed changing, and he was willing to do something about it. First, he listened to wise counsel. And second, he followed through.

So Moses *listened* to his father-in-law, and did all that he had said. *And Moses chose* able men out of all Israel, and made them heads over the people, leaders of thousands, of hundreds, of fifties and of tens. (vv. 24–25, emphasis added)

Moses matched the job to the person's abilities—some were able to lead thousands, others just a handful. But each took a share of the load, and the result was a success.

And they judged the people at all times; the difficult dispute they would bring to Moses, but every minor dispute they themselves would judge. (v. 26)

These people were not chosen because they were willing to do the work or because they were the most popular, but because their attitudes and abilities matched the tasks to be done. Moses' load was lightened, burnout was left begging at the door, and harmony prevailed in Israel's camp.

Reminders to Those Who Select Leaders

Here are three principles to help you evaluate how you can properly select leaders in your church.

The selection of officers and pastoral staff is a serious business.

The positions of leadership within a church are not to be given or taken lightly. Study the qualifications Paul lists in Titus 1:5–9.

> Set in order what remains, and appoint elders in every city as I directed you, namely, if any man be above reproach, the husband of one wife, having children who believe, not accused of dissipation or rebellion. For the overseer must be above reproach as God's steward, not self-willed, not quick-tempered, not addicted to wine, not pugnacious, not fond of sordid gain, but hospitable, loving what is good, sensible, just, devout, self-controlled, holding fast the faithful word which is in accordance with the teaching, that he may be able both to exhort in sound doctrine and to refute those who contradict.

If the church is to be effectively led, effective leaders must be chosen according to the guidelines established in Scripture. Character, not popularity, reflects God's criteria for leaders.

Those who become leaders automatically become models.

Hebrews 13:7 encourages us to study our leaders' lives.

> Remember those who led you, who spoke the word of God to you; and considering the result of their conduct, imitate their faith.

It is not good enough for officers, pastors, and leaders to simply serve efficiently in some area of responsibility; models are needed! Models who can instruct us. Models who can inspire us. Models we can imitate.

Those we select, we must willingly follow.

Our leaders will impact us and our families for years to come. They will offer us counsel and direction according to the kind of people they are. Selecting good leaders makes for peace and order in the days ahead.

> Obey your leaders, and submit to them; for they keep watch over your souls, as those who will give an account. Let them do this with joy and not with grief, for this would be unprofitable for you. (Heb. 13:17)

Significant ministries are sustained by faithful, consistent, dedicated leadership, the kind modeled by men and women in Scripture who served with integrity, refusing to lag behind because of pressure, demands, or ingratitude.

As you step into leadership or help select those who will serve, take time to examine and apply God's principles regarding character. And remember Jethro's advice—seek ways to lighten your leaders' loads. That way, they'll become more effective, and the body will become better equipped.

 ## Living Insights STUDY ONE

In John 12:21, some Greeks coming to Jerusalem to observe the Passover asked one of Jesus' disciples, "Sir, we wish to see Jesus."

In essence, the whole dying world in all its frenzied search for love and meaning is pleading this same question, knowingly or unknowingly. But where is Jesus today? How can anyone see Him?

The Scriptures teach that *we* are to be His representatives—that everyone who knows the Lord Jesus as Savior is being transformed into His likeness. Nowhere should He be more evident than in the lives of the leaders of His church. As Gene Getz has said, "A person who has become a man of God through a process of spiritual growth and development over a period of time . . . has learned to reflect Jesus Christ in his total life-style."[2]

Let's take a moment to examine the specific character traits of a Christlike leader. Read Titus 1:5–9 and 1 Timothy 3:1–7, and list the traits you find there.

Category   **Christlike Traits**

Character   _____

                          _____

2. Gene A. Getz, *The Measure of a Man* (Glendale, Calif.: G/L Publications, Regal Books, 1974), p. 16.

Family _____

Maturity _____

Reputation _____

In your own words, summarize the characteristics a qualified leader should exhibit.

_____

_____

_____

_____

 Living Insights

It's an old truth that our lives are shaped and molded by who or what we love. As Christians seeking to love God with all our hearts, souls, minds, and strength, our view of leadership should be growing more and more like His.

- Read Mark 10:42–45 and John 13:3–17, and answer the question, What is Christ's mark of a good leader?

_____

Are you exhibiting Christlike leadership in your home, church, and workplace? In the space provided, brainstorm some practical ways you can lead more effectively.

Home _____

_____

Work _____

_____

Church _____

_____

Continued on next page

65

Digging Deeper

Because leadership is such serious business, potential church officers and pastoral staff would be wise to carefully read through a statement of commitment, similar to the one below, and be able to say "I will" after each statement.

Statement of Commitment

- I recognize that the Lord, my God, is responsible for my appointment to this place of leadership. I will therefore fulfill my responsibilities as His representative, listening to His Word and obeying His voice.

- Over all other suggestions and advice, I will seek the counsel of Almighty God, as revealed in the Scriptures, in every major decision connected with my involvement in this ministry.

- I will take refuge in and rely on the Spirit of God rather than my own flesh and skill or that of any other person. I will make every effort to carry out the leadership of this position under the full control of the Holy Spirit. With my whole heart, I will fear the Lord Jesus Christ, my God, and acknowledge Him as the sovereign Head of this church, because He alone is deserving of my unreserved faithfulness, submission, diligence, and commitment. I will honor His name.

- Realizing the strong tendency to compromise with this commitment, I openly declare my dependency on God and my need for others in His family. As a servant of the Lord's body, His church, I will guard against every enemy of godly leadership—authoritarianism, exclusiveness, greed, sensuality, hypocrisy, pride, rationalization, unaccountability—and I will fulfill my responsibilities for the greater glory and praise of my Master, Jesus Christ, whom I love and willingly obey.

Chapter 9

WHY ARE WE SO BLESSED?

Psalms 103, 67

I magine yourself on a mountaintop, removed from the city concrete. God's creation stands out in bold relief: majestic clouds bleached white, fluffed against a deep blue sky; mountains rise and fall in the distance, some snowcapped, others covered with green timber; and far below, thin ribbons of water reflect the sun's warm touch as they dance through rocky ravines toward thirsty reservoirs. The elevation changes your perspective, and you see your own life as if from a distance—all that God has given you is as clear as your view of creation. A song wells up within, and your heart soars with praise to God.

> Bless the Lord, O my soul;
> And all that is within me, bless His holy name.
> Bless the Lord, O my soul,
> And forget none of His benefits. (Ps. 103:1–2)

What blessings come to mind as you close your eyes and feel the crispness of the air, the wind tugging at your clothing? Clear your thoughts of city smog and be reminded of the clean skies of God's grace.

For a While, Count Your Blessings

Have you stopped to count the blessings in your life lately? Many of us have a tendency to focus on what's wrong, which gives us a distorted picture of life—as Barry Siegel shows.

> Consider what some scientists predict.
> If everyone keeps stacking National Geographics in garages and attics instead of throwing them away, the magazines' weight will sink the continent 100 feet sometime soon and we will all be inundated by the oceans.
> If the number of microscope specimen slides submitted to one St. Louis hospital lab continues to increase at its current rate, that metropolis will be buried under three feet of glass by the year 2224.

If beachgoers keep returning home with as much sand clinging to them as they do now, 80% of the country's coastline will disappear in 10 years. . . .

[They have also] reported the striking discovery that pickles cause cancer, communism, airline tragedies, auto accidents and crime waves. About 99.9% of cancer victims had eaten pickles sometime in their lives. . . . So have 100% of all soldiers, 96.8% of communist sympathizers and 99.7% of those involved in car and air accidents. Moreover, those born in 1839 who ate pickles have suffered a 100% mortality rate. And rats force-fed 20 pounds of pickles a day for a month ended up with bulging abdomens and loss of appetite.[1]

In Psalm 103, David straightens out our picture of life by helping us see the many things we have to be thankful for, such as spiritual and physical *health* (v. 3):

[God] pardons all your iniquities;
[He] heals all your diseases;

home and family (v. 4):

[He] redeems your life from the pit;
[He] crowns you with lovingkindness and compassion;

happiness (v. 5):

[He] satisfies your years with good things,
So that your youth is renewed like the eagle;

hope (vv. 10–11):

He has not dealt with us according to our sins,
Nor rewarded us according to our iniquities.
For as high as the heavens are above the earth,
So great is His lovingkindness toward those who fear Him;

and *heritage* (vv. 17–18):

But the lovingkindness of the Lord is from everlasting
    to everlasting on those who fear Him,
And His righteousness to children's children,
To those who keep His covenant,
And who remember His precepts to do them.

1. Barry Siegel, "World May End With a Splash," *Los Angeles Times*, October 9, 1982.

"Bless the Lord, O my soul!" the psalmist exclaims as he finishes surveying God's bounty of blessings in his life (v. 22). But as fitting as praise may be, is that all God expects us to do with His blessings?

For a Change, Ask Why

Why have we been so blessed? Why has God poured His benefits into our lives? Psalm 67 offers some penetrating insight into these questions. We may be surprised by some of the answers.

The Request for Blessing

The psalmist begins by invoking God's blessing; then he adds a musical notation, Selah, which signals us "to pause and let that sink in."

> God be gracious to us and bless us,
> And cause His face to shine upon us.   [Selah.
> (v. 1)

The Living Bible puts the last part this way: "Let your face beam with joy as you look down at us." God's children through the ages have rightly longed for the blessing of their heavenly Father.

The Purpose of Blessing

As nice as it is to relax on a mountaintop and recall how God has blessed us, that's not all blessings are for. God's blessings are never an end in themselves; they're meant to be channeled to others.

> That Thy way may be known on the earth,
> Thy salvation among all nations. . . .
> God blesses us,
> That all the ends of the earth may fear Him. (vv. 2, 7)

God pours out blessings to teach us of His power and grace. He displays His blessings, not to insulate His children from the woes of the world, but to attract the attention of that hurting world.

So the answer to the question "Why are we so blessed?" is a progressive one. First, so that God's ways become known. Because as they do, His salvation message becomes clear. And as people believe this message, praise follows, as naturally and as surely as sunshine follows rain. The psalmist repeats the refrain:

> Let the peoples praise Thee, O God;
> Let all the peoples praise Thee. (vv. 3, 5)

We are blessed so that God will be praised—so that salvation may be known to the ends of the earth.

The Result of Shared Blessing

Sandwiched between the refrains that repeat God's purpose is a verse of great joy.

Let the nations be glad and sing for joy;
For Thou wilt judge the peoples with uprightness,
And guide the nations on the earth.   [Selah.
(v. 4)

Think of pictures you've seen of nations without Christ. Remember the bent bodies, despairing eyes, the struggles with spiritual and economic poverty? Imagine the same scene after the gospel has touched their lives. Eyes once darkened by hopelessness begin to radiate gladness, joy, and song. Charles Haddon Spurgeon, famed English preacher of the nineteenth century, commented on this.

> Nothing creates gladness so speedily . . . as the salvation of God. Nations never will be glad till they follow the leadership of the great Shepherd; they may shift their modes of government from monarchies to republics, and from republics to communes, but they will retain their wretchedness till they bow before the Lord of all. What a sweet word is that "to sing for joy!" . . . Whole nations will do this when Jesus reigns over them in the power of his grace.[2]

For a Moment, Think of How

The final question, and a critical one, is, How do we go about carrying God's message?

We must know.

We cannot share a message we do not have. Do you know Jesus in a personal way? We must first have received the blessing before we can give it away.

> "For God so loved the world, that He gave His only begotten Son, that whoever believes in Him should not perish, but have eternal life." (John 3:16)

We must live.

We must live the message we claim to know. There should be a distinction between our lives and the lives of those without Christ.

---

2. C. H. Spurgeon, *The Treasury of David* (New York, N.Y.: Funk and Wagnalls, 1882), vol. 3, p. 206.

Do all things without grumbling or disputing; that you may prove yourselves to be blameless and innocent, children of God above reproach in the midst of a crooked and perverse generation, among whom you appear as lights in the world. (Phil. 2:14–15)

We must go.

Even when people see the difference, few will approach us to hear about our Christ. If we want them to know Him, we need to take the initiative to tell them.

"Go therefore and make disciples of all the nations, baptizing them in the name of the Father and the Son and the Holy Spirit, teaching them to observe all that I commanded you; and lo, I am with you always, even to the end of the age." (Matt. 28:19–20)

We must give.

Our material blessings are a trust with eternal consequences. When we give from those resources, God's song will be sung throughout the world.

"Then the King will say to those on His right, 'Come, you who are blessed of My Father, inherit the kingdom prepared for you from the foundation of the world. For I was hungry, and you gave Me something to eat; I was thirsty, and you gave Me drink; I was a stranger, and you invited Me in; naked, and you clothed Me; I was sick, and you visited Me; I was in prison, and you came to Me.' Then the righteous will answer Him, saying, 'Lord, when did we see You hungry, and feed You, or thirsty, and give You drink? And when did we see You a stranger, and invite You in, or naked, and clothe You? And when did we see You sick, or in prison, and come to You?' And the King will answer and say to them, 'Truly I say to you, to the extent that you did it to one of these brothers of Mine, even the least of them, you did it to Me.'" (25:34–40)

A Concluding Thought

Remember the mountaintop experience where we began to count our blessings? There is another mountaintop, an imaginary one, that may say something to those of us in the United States of America.

Consider the world as if it were shrunk down to a community of 1000 persons:
In our town of 1000—
180 of us live high on a hill called the developed world;
820 live on the rocky bottom land called the rest of the world.
The fortunate 180 on the hill have 80 percent of the wealth of the whole town, over half of all the rooms in town with over two rooms per person, 85 percent of all the automobiles, 80 percent of all the TV sets, 93 percent of all the telephones, and an average income of $5000 per person per year.
The not-so-fortunate 820 people on the bottom get by on only $700 per person per year, many of them on less than $75. They average five persons to a room.
How does the fortunate group of hill-dwellers use its incredible wealth? Well, as a group they spend less than 1 percent of their income to aid the lower land. (In the United States, for example, of every $100 earned:
$18.30 goes for food
$6.60 is spent on recreation and amusement
$5.80 buys clothes
$2.40 buys alcohol
$1.50 buys tobacco
$1.30 is given for religious and charitable uses, and only a small part of that goes outside the U.S.)
I wonder how the villagers on the crowded plain— a third of whose people are suffering from malnutrition—feel about the folks on the hill?[3]

The blessings of God may not continue to rest on us much longer, either as Christians, as a church, or as a country. But surely, if they do, the gracious way in which we give of our *own* blessings will be a major reason.

"Give, and it will be given to you; good measure, pressed down, shaken together, running over, they will pour

3. Dr. Paul Brand and Philip Yancey, *Fearfully and Wonderfully Made* (Grand Rapids, Mich.: Zondervan Publishing House, 1980), pp. 61–62.

into your lap. For by your standard of measure it will be measured to you in return." (Luke 6:38)

 ## Living Insights

A child rarely seems to appreciate a toy as much as when another tries to play with it! In a similar way we adults are often only vaguely aware of God's blessings—our health, a job, someone we love—until they have been removed from us. Let's explore this further by taking a moment to answer the following questions.

- If an attitude of thankfulness to God is absent in our lives, what might replace it?

Deuteronomy 8:11–14 _____

Nehemiah 9:16–17 _____

Job 2:7–10 _____

Numbers 11 _____

- In light of the previous passages, combined with your own experience, how do you think a lack of thankfulness affects your relationship with God?

_____

_____

_____

_____

- With others?

_____

_____

_____

_____

As you can see, an attitude of thankfulness is an indispensable part of a healthy relationship with God and others. Psalm 105:5 says, "Remember His wonders which He has done, / His marvels, and the judgments uttered by His mouth."

Here are a couple of suggestions to help you nurture an attitude of thankfulness. *First*, on a separate piece of paper write out a few specific blessings you can thank God for—your home, family, salvation, a particular aspect of God's character, and so on. Put this list somewhere highly visible, like on your refrigerator or in your car, to help you get into the practice of thanking God for His blessings. *Second*, think of someone in your life whom God has used to bless you. Have you forgotten to thank this person? Make plans to do so now.

🍇 Living Insights   STUDY TWO

Many benefits of God's blessings go far beyond the blessings themselves. Joshua 3:14–4:24 provides us with an excellent example of this. Take a moment to read the account.

Now you are ready to mine even deeper for the wealth available in God's blessings. As we sift through the passage, we will find two stated and two implied benefits of remembering God's blessings.

Stated Benefits

- *Remembering God's blessings enables us to teach future generations.* Joshua 4:21–25 explains how the stones will serve as a visual object lesson parents could use to tutor their children, teaching them about God by recalling His past blessings. By remembering, we can create opportunities to teach our own families about God and His work in our lives.

- *Remembering God's blessings reminds us that we should fear God.* Joshua said in 4:24, "That all the peoples of the earth may know that the hand of the Lord is mighty, so that you may fear the Lord your God forever." If we forget how God miraculously intervenes in our lives, we will lose the sense of awe that is so vital to a pure relationship with Him.

Implied Benefits

- *Remembering God's blessings imparts a crucial sense of belonging to God and of being a uniquely called people.* Can you imagine an Israelite who was not overwhelmed with the feeling of belonging to God after walking on dry land . . . through the rolled-back Jordan River? What Israelite, stepping out of the riverbed onto the Promised Land with thousands of others, felt like part of just any ordinary tribe of people? By remembering, we can reaffirm to ourselves and to our children the truths that we belong to God and that we're all members of His body (1 Cor. 12:27).

- *Remembering God's blessings nourishes our faith.* Just as it was God's past faithfulness that gave David the confidence to fight Goliath (1 Sam. 17, esp. vv. 34–37), so these stones of remembrance gave Israel confidence to go forward regardless of how deep, how broad, or how swift the rivers that lay in their future.

Here's a practical suggestion to help you remember God's blessings in your life. Right along with those important scrapbooks that hold cherished family photos, begin a family "memory book" that records God's blessings. Each member of the family could contribute once a month, or maybe every three months—you decide. Then, at least once a year, reap the benefits of God's blessings by sitting down together to remember God's kindnesses in your life.

Chapter 10

WHAT IS MY RESPONSE TO GOD'S BLESSINGS?

Matthew 25:14–30

S ome things in life are optional and some are not." So writes C. Peter Wagner in his book, *On the Crest of the Wave.* He continues,

> Wearing shoes is optional. But eating is not.
>
> Driving a car is optional. But once you choose the option, driving on the right hand side of the road (here in America) is not. . . .
>
> I'm not saying that these things are impossible. You can choose to go without eating, but if you do you must take the consequences. You must be willing to exist at a low energy level, to invite infection and disease, and, if you persist, to die.
>
> You can choose to drive on the left but you will pay fines and cause accidents.[1]

In the Christian life, we have the option of being good stewards with the blessings God has given us, or using His gifts with only our own aims in sight. We are free to choose either response. But we must be aware that each choice has its own set of consequences, just like driving on the right- or left-hand side of the street. Let's explore this further in our chapter today.

Reminders regarding God's Blessings

Let's review a few general truths about God's blessings in our lives.

God's blessings are numerous and varied.

They come in abundance, in different shapes, sizes, times, ages, and stages.

God's blessings are beyond what we deserve.

Every time God pours out His blessings, we receive the good gifts He wants us to have, never what our sinfulness deserves. All His blessings come under the heading of grace and mercy.

1. C. Peter Wagner, *On the Crest of the Wave* (Ventura, Calif.: GL Publications, Regal Books, 1983), p. 5.

God's blessings are poured out on the just as well as the unjust.

Matthew 5:45b tells us,

> "He causes His sun to rise on the evil and the good,
> and sends rain on the righteous and the unrighteous."

A Christian farmer and his non-Christian neighbor, for example, each receive from the same storm, the same sky, and the same God. The common graces of God fall upon both—the difference is in the recipients' response.

God's blessings have a purpose.

As we learned in the previous chapter, God blesses us in order to draw attention to His grace and mercy. He blesses the just so that His saving power is sent around the world. He blesses the unjust so that they might respond positively to His offer of salvation. Matthew 25 records a story told by Jesus that shows how different people respond to God's blessings and how their choices impact their lives.

A Story: Right and Wrong Responses

As we turn to this story, we need to step back in time, slip on some sandals, and listen to Jesus speak. It will not be long before Jesus is arrested, pushed through a kangaroo court on trumped-up charges of blasphemy and treason, and finally crucified. His impending death prompts Him to prepare His disciples for His absence and return. His method of communication is storytelling, through the use of a parable.[2]

A Foundational Statement

The basis of the story is found in Matthew 24:42 (see also 25:13):

> "Therefore be on the alert, for you do not know which
> day your Lord is coming."

It's an urgent warning. Jesus' disciples dare not live hoping to somehow "phase into" His arrival or to receive a special sign just before the hour arrives. To help them understand the implications of this warning, He tells a story that falls neatly into four parts.

The Master's Provisions and Departure

The story begins.

> "For it is just like a man about to go on a journey, who
> called his own slaves, and entrusted his possessions to

---

2. The word *parable* is a compound word made up of *para*, meaning "alongside" and *ballō*, meaning "to throw." A parable teaches unknown truth by throwing it alongside known information for the purpose of comparison.

them. And to one he gave five talents, to another, two, and to another, one, each according to his own ability; and he went on his journey." (vv. 14–15)

Aside from the master who is leaving and the slaves who are staying, the only significant thing in these verses is the master's possessions. And these are called talents, which we normally think of as natural abilities. But in Jesus' day, the talent was a standard of weight to measure the value of a coin—the man was distributing his riches among his slaves for safekeeping.

The Slaves' Response and Report

While the man is gone, his slaves decide individually how best to handle their responsibilities.

"Immediately the one who had received the five talents went and traded with them, and gained five more talents. In the same manner the one who had received the two talents gained two more. But he who received the one talent went away and dug in the ground, and hid his master's money." (vv. 16–18)

Each slave invests and doubles his money—except the last slave. He just buries it in a safe place. But in verse 19, the day of reckoning comes, and the master wants a report of each man's stewardship.

"Now after a long time the master of those slaves came and settled accounts with them. And the one who had received the five talents came up and brought five more talents, saying, 'Master, you entrusted five talents to me; see, I have gained five more talents.' . . . The one also who had received the two talents came up and said, 'Master, you entrusted to me two talents; see, I have gained two more talents.' . . . And the one also who had received the one talent came up and said, 'Master, I knew you to be a hard man, reaping where you did not sow, and gathering where you scattered no seed. And I was afraid, and went away and hid your talent in the ground; see, you have what is yours.'" (vv. 19–20, 22, 24–25)

The Master's Reaction and Evaluation

After each report, the master makes a comment to each slave. To the first two men he says,

"'Well done, good and faithful slave; you were faithful with a few things, I will put you in charge of many things, enter into the joy of your master.'" (v. 21; see also v. 23)

It's not often that we see in Scripture two identical verses, and in this case, the repetition is especially significant. We would tend to think the five-talent man's reward would be different from the reward of the two-talent man. Yet the master's response to them is identical. The issue was not how much each of them had been given; the issue was what they had done with what they had. That truth is made even more clear in the master's response to the third man.

> "'You wicked, lazy slave, you knew that I reap where I did not sow, and gather where I scattered no seed. Then you ought to have put my money in the bank, and on my arrival I would have received my money back with interest. Therefore take away the talent from him, and give it to the one who has the ten talents.'" (vv. 26–28)

The slave had known what his boss expected. He had no excuse. He simply ignored what he knew to be true—that one day he would have to give account for his area of responsibility.

General Principle and Final Rebuke

In every parable there is a primary lesson to be learned. In this one, Jesus wanted His disciples to know that in His absence they would be entrusted with responsibilities for which they would one day give an account. But this parable has a message for us too—that God's blessings call for a response. His blessings come in different sizes and shapes, but they never come without an expectation of return. Those who respond correctly to God's blessings enjoy the benefit of His approval. But those who deny their responsibilities reap negative consequences. Verse 30 makes that clear.

> "And cast out the worthless slave into the outer darkness; in that place there shall be weeping and gnashing of teeth."

The phrases "outer darkness" and "weeping and gnashing of teeth" refer to eternal condemnation.[3] The third slave illustrates the terrible consequences that fall upon a person who rejects God's grace, which has been offered through Jesus Christ.

3. Throughout Scripture these phrases refer only to those who are eternally lost. Another explanation of the "outer darkness" is that it is the opposite of "the joy inside." "The faithful servants enter into the joy of their Lord. The unfaithful servant is excluded from that joy." Zane C. Hodges, Grace in Eclipse (Dallas, Tex.: Redención Viva, 1985), p. 93.

How Does All This Relate to Me?

The story has unfolded, the truths have been examined, and we've seen that our sovereign blessings are serious business. This relates directly to each of us in at least four ways.

There are no special categories of slaves.

All three men in the story are referred to equally as slaves. There are no superslaves, vocational slaves, lay slaves, or clergy slaves. We are all just ordinary people, same rank, same title. The only real difference is in how we respond to our Master's blessings.

No slave is taken advantage of.

God gives to "each according to his own ability" (v. 15). Isn't this a great relief from frustration and guilt? We're not all given the same abilities, but we're each given responsibilities in line with our skills. Some of us can preach, some can sing, others can evangelize or give large sums of money. Others may have vision, be able to motivate others, start schools, dream creatively, write books, or found churches. But God gives each of us the abilities He wants us to have. He always gives us exactly what we can handle—never too much or too little. We'd be wise, then, not to compare ourselves to others but rather to measure our activities by our own abilities.[4]

Whenever the Master entrusts, He will also expect and inspect.

Give these phrases some thought: "entrusted his possessions" (v. 14); "you entrusted . . . to me" (v. 20; see also v. 22); "you ought to have put my money in the bank" (v. 27).

God means for us to enjoy the taste of His blessings. But to selfishly gorge ourselves on them is to misunderstand His intentions.

> "And from everyone who has been given much shall
> much be required; and to whom they entrusted much,
> of him they will ask all the more." (Luke 12:48b)

God gives to us graciously, and when He does, He holds us accountable for the gifts He has given. "It is required of stewards that one be found trustworthy" (1 Cor. 4:2).[5]

What are your gifts from the Lord? Life? Children? Finances? Salvation? Are you using these gifts selfishly? Or faithfully, as a steward who must give an account?

4. See 2 Corinthians 10:12–13.

5. A steward manages another person's possessions. In this case, all Christians are responsible to manage the things given to them by God.

The slave's response may be optional, but the Master's is not.

All of our decisions begin as options, but each choice bears its own inevitable consequences. The Master will not say to every person in the last day, "Well done, good and faithful slave" (Matt. 25:21, 23). He will, however, reward those who have been good stewards of His blessings. And He will do as He has said. Therefore, consider why God has blessed you, and "be on the alert then, for you do not know the day nor the hour" (v. 13).

🍇 Living Insights

In Matthew 13:45–46, Jesus says that the kingdom of heaven is like a merchant looking for fine pearls, and once he finds a pearl of great value, he sells all that he has to buy it. Juan Carlos Ortiz, in his book *Call to Discipleship*, amplifies this parable for us.

> According to traditional thinking, man is the pearl . . . and Jesus the merchant. . . . Now I understand that *He* is the pearl of great price, and man the merchant.
>
> So when man finds Jesus, . . . [he] marvels at such a pearl and says, "I want this pearl. How much does it cost?" . . .
>
> "It costs everything you have—no more, no less—so anybody can buy it."
>
> "I'll buy it."
>
> "What do you have? Let's write it down."
>
> "I have $10,000 in the bank."
>
> "Good, $10,000. What else?"
>
> "I have nothing more. That's all I have." . . .
>
> "Where do you live?"
>
> "I live in my house."
>
> "The house too." . . .
>
> "Do you mean that I must live in my car, then?"
>
> "Have you a car?"
>
> "I have two."
>
> "Both become mine. Both cars. What else?" . . .
>
> "I have nothing else."
>
> "Are you alone in the world?"
>
> "No, I have a wife, two children. . . ."
>
> "Your wife and your children too."
>
> "Too?"
>
> "Yes, everything you have. What else?"

"I have nothing else, I am left alone now."

"Oh, you too. Everything. Everything becomes mine. . . . Now you can use all those things here but don't forget they are mine, as you are. When I need any of the things you are using you must give them to me because now I am the owner."[6]

God says we have been bought with a price—the blood of Christ purchased our salvation. We are no longer owners but debtors. Every blessing from God, even our very lives, is no longer ours to do with as we see fit, but as the new owner desires.

And He died for all, that they who live should no longer live for themselves, but for Him who died and rose again on their behalf. (2 Cor. 5:15)

Is there a particular possession, attitude, or ability that you are hoping to keep hidden from the Master because of selfishness? Is it possible that you are keeping certain things buried, like the unfaithful steward in Matthew 25, so that they are not under the Master's control?

If you find yourself answering yes to these questions, spend some time now confessing these "buried blessings" before God. Ask for His forgiveness and guidance in helping you discover how He wants them used. Space has been provided for you to write down some of your thoughts.

_____

_____

_____

_____

_____

_____

_____

_____

_____

_____

6. Juan Carlos Ortiz, as told to Jamie Buckingham, Call to Discipleship (Plainfield, N.J.: Logos International, 1975), pp. 42–43.

One of the biggest fears we have of putting our lives under God's control is fear of the unknown: What will happen if . . .

> I give Him control over my marriage?
> I give Him control over my money?
> I give Him control over my job?

Before we entrust anything of value to someone, we like to know what that person's going to do with it. Our hesitancy to give God control stems from the same issue. Deep in our hearts we wrestle with the questions, Can we *really* trust Him? Can we *really* believe He will always act out of His love toward us?

Only as we become convinced that He is trustworthy will our fear of giving Him control dissipate. Only then can we give Him unreserved ownership—not because we know where it will all lead, but because we truly trust the One in control.

The following Scriptures can help bolster your trust in God if you are willing to invest some time reading, praying, and meditating over them.

Romans 8:28–39   Ephesians 2:4–7   Psalm 139:1–12

Chapter 11

HOW SHOULD WE INTERPRET GOD'S CALENDAR?

Matthew 24:3–14

P robably no one lives by the calendar as much as farmers do. Each season brings a task that can't be put off: spring's melting snow and thawing ground won't wait for a convenient time to plant; summer's foraging insects demand daily combat; autumn's crisp air hurries a harvest that won't wait; and winter's icy breath brings its own set of emergencies.

Farmers must be sensitive to changing seasons or else the entire harvest could be lost. Unlike the farmer, however, most Christians are sadly insensitive to the brisk winds of God's end-time calendar. We don't realize that time is running out for those without Christ, and that their eternity is at stake.

Scripture urges the fellow workers in God's field to get on with the task of reaping the world for Christ. But why is work in the mission field so urgent? Matthew 24:42 provides the answer.

"Be on the alert, for you do not know which day your Lord is coming."

Our sense of urgency comes because Christ's return is not only certain but imminent—it may come any year, any hour, any moment.

As God pulls off another page of His calendar, let's be aware of the change in seasons. Let's feel the crisp air that harbingers the end times. And let's look up, with a farmer's sense of urgency, at fields that are ripe and waiting to be harvested.

Promise and Fulfillment

Between a promise and its fulfillment, there are times of doubt— especially if the fulfillment is a long time in coming. Remember General Douglas MacArthur's promise on Corregidor to the Philippine people? On March 11, 1942, the general was leaving the Philippines to establish another front in the South Pacific. But just before he left, he spoke the words that echo in almost every history textbook,

"I shall return." He didn't tell them when; in his case, he didn't know. But two-and-a-half years later, on October 20, 1944, he waded ashore and announced, "I have returned. By the grace of Almighty God, our forces stand again on Philippine soil."

The Philippine people must have wondered if MacArthur would ever return to liberate their islands. He did return; but had the tide of the war gone against the Allies, his word would have sunk in the Pacific, a water-logged promise. But Jesus' word is infallible. He will return, regardless of human events or opinions (see John 14:1–3). In the interim, however, questions and doubts may plague us.

Like us, the disciples also had questions about the future.

The Disciples' Questions

Matthew 24 opens with the disciples seeking to speak with Jesus privately. They want to know how they'll recognize Jesus' return, so, understandably, they ply Him with questions.

> "When will these things be, and what will be the sign
> of Your coming, and of the end of the age?" (v. 3b)

The Lord's Answers

Jesus responds with an answer that unfolds throughout Matthew 24. It includes a warning, signs to watch for, and predictable end-time results.

A warning. Jesus prefaces His response with an admonition.

> Jesus answered and said to them, "See to it that no
> one misleads you." (v. 4)

In other words, "Don't be deceived." This warning occurs no less than ten times in the New Testament. During Jesus' absence, misinformation will wither our sense of urgency and breed doubts about the imminency of His return. Second Peter 3:3–4 adds to Jesus' admonition.

> Know this first of all, that in the last days mockers will
> come with their mocking, following after their own
> lusts, and saying, "Where is the promise of His com-
> ing? For ever since the fathers fell asleep, all continues
> just as it was from the beginning of creation."

Before these mockers ever darken the horizon of the prophetic scene, Jesus points them out so that we won't be deceived.

> "For many will come in My name, saying, 'I am the
> Christ,' and will mislead many." (Matt. 24:5)

85

Signs to watch for. The opposite extreme of being naively misled is to read prophetical significance into every detail of life. The nightly news and the morning paper cast long shadows of fear in the minds of believers who are anticipating the end times. But these are merely foreshadowings of a darker night yet to come—they're not the night itself.

> "And you will be hearing of wars and rumors of wars; see that you are not frightened, for those things must take place, but *that is not yet the end.*" (v. 6, emphasis added)

As long as there are two people on earth, there will be fights. Whether between two children or two nations, wars are part and parcel of human existence. But these events do not signal the end.

> "For nation will rise against nation, and kingdom against kingdom, and in various places there will be famines and earthquakes. But all these things are merely the beginning of birth pangs." (vv. 7–8)

Jesus calls these global upheavals "birth pangs," the beginning contractions of labor. The analogy is a good one, for although there is pain, there is also hope for the birth of a new kingdom. In verse 9, Jesus moves from global signs to more personal ones. The first is the persecution of Christians.

> "Then they will deliver you to tribulation, and will kill you, and you will be hated by all nations on account of My name."

As the end of time approaches, there will be a growing dislike and even hatred of Christians.[1] Apostasy and polarization, and even betrayal within the Christian community itself, will characterize this era.

> "And at that time many will fall away and will deliver up one another and hate one another." (v. 10)

In verse 11, we find another sign.

> "And many false prophets will arise, and will mislead many."

---

1. It is difficult to calculate the numbers of Christians who have died as a result of antagonistic political and social ideologies in the past, but persecution appears on the increase. Winrich Scheffbuch documents some of these in *Christians Under the Hammer and Sickle,* trans. Mark A. Noll (Grand Rapids, Mich.: Zondervan Publishing House, 1974), as does Carl Lawrence in *The Church in China* (Minneapolis, Minn.: Bethany House Publishers, 1985).

These prophets are different from the false Christs mentioned in verse 5. A false Christ claims to be the Messiah. False prophets don't make that claim, but instead peddle false teachings. They are the leaders of all the cults and isms. These religion vendors promise a change of life, but one that utterly ignores the significance of Jesus.

Predictable end-time results. On the negative side, the end times will be a moral ice age.

> "And because lawlessness is increased, most people's love will grow cold." (v. 12)

On the positive side, true believers will survive that winter by their loyalty to Christ.

> "But the one who endures to the end, he shall be saved." (v. 13)[2]

And because of their enduring faith, Jesus says that the gospel will thaw patches of humanity in the farthest corners of the world.

> "And this gospel of the kingdom shall be preached in the whole world for a witness to all the nations, and then the end shall come." (v. 14)

Outreach is a task assigned to the church by Christ, but it's easy to lose our sense of urgency when we lose sight of the overall picture.

> I am reminded of the digging of the Panama Canal. Over a period of decades, several major attempts failed to finish the job. Finally, one effort carved through the isthmus. . . .
>
> How sad the worker who shoveled away without seeing the big picture. How foolish the Yankee laborer who may have been tempted to settle in an improved Panama with railroads and drained swamps and forget about the canal he had been sent to build! This sort of short-sightedness was, in part, why previous efforts failed.
>
> And how sad the Christian who lovingly spreads good news, but without a conviction that God's global purposes are to be accomplished.[3]

---

2. For another interpretation see Zane C. Hodges' *Grace in Eclipse* (Dallas, Tex.: Redención Viva, 1985), pp. 102–4.

3. Steve Hawthorne, "Penetrating the Last Frontiers," *World Christian*, March/April 1983, p. 10.

What Is Needed?

Why is reaching the world for Christ so urgent? Because people are of utmost importance, and because the sun is westering away on human history. But to gain God's sense of urgency, we need to do two things—understand God's part in history and get involved in it!

We need to understand the theme and goal of history.

It's impossible for us to have God's perfect perspective on the events of the world, but we must remember this: God is central in the unfolding of these events.

> The meaning of history is a problem which is today confounding the minds of thinking men. . . .
>
> In a former generation, the philosophy of progress was widely accepted. Some thinkers charted the meaning of history by a single straight line which traced a gradual but steady incline from primitive savage beginnings upward to a high level of culture and civilization. . . .
>
> Other interpretations have been utterly pessimistic. Someone has suggested that the most accurate chart of the meaning of history is the set of tracks made by a drunken fly with feet wet with ink, staggering across a piece of white paper. They lead nowhere and reflect no pattern of meaning. . . .
>
> . . . It is the author's conviction that the ultimate meaning of history must be found in the action of God in history as recorded and interpreted in inspired Scripture. . . . God has been redemptively at work in history; and the divine action will yet bring history to a divinely destined goal.[4]

We need to be involved in the action.

How do we develop a sense of urgency for a world without Christ? The first step is to *catch a world vision* by understanding that Jesus didn't die for a race of people or for a country, but for the world. The *entire* world, as the song says: "Red and yellow, black and white, / They are precious in His sight— / Jesus loves the little children of the world."[5]

---

4. George Eldon Ladd, *The Gospel of the Kingdom* (Grand Rapids, Mich.: William B. Eerdmans Publishing Co., 1959), pp. 130–32.

5. "Jesus Loves the Little Children," *Hymns for the Family of God* (Nashville, Tenn.: Paragon Associates, 1976), no. 15.

The second step we must take is to *keep a world vision*. And we do that by continually rubbing shoulders with passionate, visionary Christians who will, in turn, kindle our passion for the mission field.

The third step is to *obey a world vision*. There are no desk jobs for farmers. We must be out in the fields, sweating together, laboring together . . . hand in hand . . . heart in heart.

So many of the metaphors Jesus uses to describe the kingdom are taken from agriculture—the parable of the soils, the parable of the mustard seed, the parable of the wheat and tares.

Similarly, the words of Christ to His disciples in John 4 employ another image from the world of agriculture—

> "Do you not say, 'There are yet four months, and then comes the harvest'? Behold, I say to you, lift up your eyes, and look on the fields, that they are white for harvest." (v. 35)

It's easy for us to sit back and lose a sense of urgency for the work of God. It's easy for us to say there's plenty of time to tell our neighbors about Christ . . . or our relatives . . . or the people we work with. Surely there are "yet four months" before the harvest . . .

But we never know when God will tear the last page from His prophetic calendar, and we never know when the Grim Reaper will come for a final harvest of his own.

Living Insights   STUDY ONE

If someone were to ask you how many red cars you saw while driving today, what would you answer—one, two? Maybe you would think, "Hmm, there must have been several," but you'd be unable to remember any specifically.

But what if this same person offered to pay you fifty dollars for every red car you saw the next time you were driving. How many do you think you would notice then? All of them! The difference, of course, is that where before you had no real reason to notice red cars, now you do.

Our view of non-Christians works much the same way. Normally, many of us cruise leisurely through life, focusing mainly on the road ahead, not really aware of those in the other lanes. But Christ's return should motivate us not only to see but to even seek out those passing all around us without Christ—before it is too late.

Use the following questions to evaluate the effect Christ's return is having in your life.

- Is there more urgency in my pursuit of money, things, and prestige than in my efforts to share Christ with others?

- How do I see people? Educated or uneducated, popular or unpopular, rich or poor? Or do I look beyond those exteriors for dying people in need of a Savior?

If fifty dollars is sufficient motivation to see the red cars we might normally miss, how much more should Christ's imminent return create a sense of urgency for seeking those who are lost?

 **Living Insights**   STUDY TWO

Just for fun, count how many *f*s you see in the following statement.

FINISHED FILES ARE THE RE-
SULT OF YEARS OF SCIENTIF-
IC STUDY COMBINED WITH THE
EXPERIENCE OF MANY YEARS.

How many did you find? If your answer was three, you might want to count again. All together there are six!

This simple exercise points out how easily we can think we see everything and yet still miss something. It's a crucial element to any con man's game—gaining your trust by convincing you that you see everything, when all you really see is what he wants you to see. Jesus warns in Matthew 24:4, "See to it that no one misleads you"—don't be deceived by the religious impostors to come. The one pulling the strings of these puppet prophets is Satan, the father of lies.

However, besides being deceived by others, we can also deceive ourselves—through denial, rationalization, and blame. Think of the fellow who told the judge he wasn't to blame for killing the man he was trying to rob, "because if he'd given me the money, I wouldn't have had to shoot him." We can't always trust only in our human wisdom to tell us what is true.

So if we can't always trust others or ourselves, how can we guard against being deceived?

Open your Bibles and carefully read the following references. Then answer the question, How can we keep from being misled?

John 14:16–21 _____

_____

_____

Psalm 19:7–11 _____

_____

_____

John 8:31–32 _____

_____

_____

Chapter 12

WHY DO WE THROW ROCKS AT EACH OTHER?

Ephesians 4:25–32

T hree centuries before Christ, a Greek philosopher named Bion used an insightful image to teach a timeless truth.

Though boys throw stones at frogs in sport, the frogs do not die in sport, but in earnest.[1]

Picture the scene. Boys playing on the bank of some tranquil pond . . . spotting a few plump frogs on a cluster of lily pads . . . filling their hands with sharp-cornered rocks . . . taking careful aim . . . then launching their surprise attack.

A few of the frogs escape, diving for safety. Those who are hit die a painful death as their lifeblood slowly ebbs away.

Just a little afternoon's sport, right?

Maybe for the boys. Certainly not for the frogs. For the frogs, it's a matter of life and death.

Sadly, even as adults, we still stand on the banks and throw stones. Only instead of throwing stones at frogs, we aim sharp-cornered words at each other.

For some, these verbal stones are thrown in sarcastic sport. For others, in an angry vendetta. And for still others, in self-righteous indignation—like the religious leaders who stood ready to stone the adulterous woman in John 8.

In today's study we want to explore the question: Why do we throw rocks at each other? To help us answer this question, we'll turn to Ephesians 4:25–32, where Paul shares some penetrating insights into the believer's nature.

Four Contrasts That Warn Us

In the preceding verses, Paul has just talked about the old and new natures every Christian possesses. Like garments, these two

---

1. Bion, as quoted in *Bartlett's Familiar Quotations*, 14th ed., rev. and enl., ed. Emily Morison Beck (Boston, Mass.: Little, Brown and Co., 1968), p. 104.

natures hang in the inner closet of our life—the repugnant one of our fallen nature and the resplendent one that Jesus has given us. Paul urges us to "lay aside the old self" (v. 22) and "put on the new self" (v. 24). Then, as if he's choosing our wardrobe, he lists what is fitting for a Christian to wear and what isn't.

First: *Instead of lying, speak the truth.*

> Therefore, laying aside falsehood, speak truth, each one of you, with his neighbor, for we are members of one another. (v. 25)

Second: *Instead of allowing anger to linger, resolve it.*

> Be angry, and yet do not sin; do not let the sun go down on your anger, and do not give the devil an opportunity. (vv. 26–27)

Third: *Instead of stealing, work hard.*

> Let him who steals steal no longer; but rather let him labor, performing with his own hands what is good, in order that he may have something to share with him who has need. (v. 28)

Fourth: *Instead of speaking destructively, speak constructively.*

> Let no unwholesome word proceed from your mouth, but only such a word as is good for edification according to the need of the moment, that it may give grace to those who hear. (v. 29)

Lies, lingering anger, theft, and hurtful speech are the stained, tattered, and ill-fitting wardrobe of our old nature. Living our life indigently wrapped in those rags is ludicrous when we've got such a beautiful set of new clothes easily within reach: truth, peace, diligence, and encouragement.

Every time we dig back into the dark recesses of that closet to pull out one of those old garments, it grieves the very One who washed us and gave us those new clothes.

> And do not grieve the Holy Spirit of God, by whom you were sealed for the day of redemption. (v. 30)

Take a good look in a full-length mirror for a moment, will you? What do you see? Are your clothes fit for the presence of a King? Or are they fit only for the shadowed alleyways of life?

Six Negatives That Tear Us Down

As Paul continues his checklist of things to be tossed in the trash, he pulls out the rags we've secreted away in our hearts.

> Let all bitterness and wrath and anger and clamor and slander be put away from you, along with all malice. (v. 31)

Bitterness

The word in the original Greek is *pikria* and refers to long-standing resentment, brooding over past offenses, harboring grudges, and rehearsing insults. To be bitter toward another person is the first step to picking up a rock. The bigger the bitterness, the bigger the rock you will hurl. And the longer you hold onto the bitterness, the more rocks you will throw.

Wrath and Anger

The Greek terms are *thumos* and *orgē*, respectively, which refer to long-lived rage. They reveal themselves in outbursts of uncontrolled passion and frustration. They're like the flames that flare up when straw is ignited; they subside quickly, then smolder.

Clamor

The Greek word is *kraugē*, which the NIV translates as "brawling." This tawdry piece of character flashes itself publicly in noisy and aggressive shouting matches during the heat of discussion.

Slander

The Greek term is *blasphēmia.* It refers to injurious speech—hurtful things often said when the other person isn't present to make a defense.

Malice

The Greek word is *kakia.* This is a general term for wickedness and depravity. Jesus uses this word in Matthew 6:34 when He says that "each day has enough *trouble* of its own" (emphasis added). And Paul uses it in 1 Corinthians 14:20 when he advises the church to "not be children in your thinking; yet in *evil* be babes, but in your thinking be mature" (emphasis added).

So many of these problems of the heart evidence themselves in our speech.

> "The good man out of the good treasure of his heart brings forth what is good; and the evil man out of the

evil treasure brings forth what is evil; for his mouth speaks from that which fills his heart." (Luke 6:45)

We can either use stones to throw at others, or we can use them as building blocks. In the same way, our words can either hurt someone or bring healing (Prov. 12:18). They can either contribute to the life of a relationship or usher in its death (18:21).

Three Positives That Build Us Up

Just as the external manifestations of our old nature begin in our heart (Mark 7:21–23), so the more visible evidences of our new nature begin there also. Paul concludes Ephesians 4 by listing three of the positive inner qualities of our new nature.

And be kind to one another, tender-hearted, forgiving each other, just as God in Christ also has forgiven you. (v. 32)

Kindness

The word is the opposite of all that is hard and sharp. Kindness hones the edges off our words and wraps them in grace. Like the words used to guard delicate things—*Fragile: Handle with Care*—a kind person is careful to handle people with gentleness and graciousness.

Tenderheartedness

The idea here is compassion. Remember how Matthew described the Lord when He saw the multitudes? "He felt compassion for them, because they were distressed and downcast like sheep without a shepherd" (Matt. 9:36). Jesus had the ability to see what those around Him didn't. He had an artist's eye to see deep within the subject being painted. He had perception into character. And into feelings. He could see into people's hearts, not only because He was God, but because He was so tenderhearted.

Forgiveness

This quality has the capacity to reach through time to the painful hurts of the past. And in reaching back, it can touch every wound with a healing ointment that is only available at the cross of Christ. There we find not only the power to forgive but also the power to forgive others as God has forgiven us. Completely. Unconditionally. And for all eternity.

The Distinguishing Marks of the Christian

Love and unity are the distinguishing marks of the Christian (see John 13:34–35, 17:21)—not black and blue marks.

We live out our faith before a watching world. What they see will be a factor in determining their eternal destiny. Quite a responsibility, isn't it? Quite an incentive to drop the rocks we so stubbornly cling to.

 Living Insights

How can we change from rock throwers who tear down into brick masons who build up? Is it merely a matter of reading the right books? No—it's not what's in our libraries that counts; it's what's in our lives. Most of us already know what we should be doing. The question is: Why aren't we doing it?

The answer is simple: We cannot give away what we do not have. The Scriptures are clear that God, through Christ, lavishes His love upon us. If we've never fully experienced that love, it's difficult to pass it on to others. So when the Lord beckons us to be kind, tenderhearted, and forgiving, He is only asking us to give others what He has already freely given us.

Take a moment to meditate on God's kindness, compassion, and forgiveness toward you. Then think of some specific ways He can use you to build up others. Inscribe them in the space provided; but more importantly, inscribe them in the lives of others.

- On the basis of the kindness I have received from Christ, what kindness can I administer to others?

_____

_____

_____

- On the basis of the compassion I have received from Christ, what compassion can I share?

_____

_____

_____

- On the basis of the forgiveness I have received from Christ, what forgiveness can I pass along?

_____

_____

_____

🍇 *Living Insights*

Now that you have reached the final stop on your journey through this series of questions, pause to look behind you. Are the vines of forgetfulness already creeping across your mind, making it difficult to recall what you have learned?

In his book *How to Improve Your Memory,* James D. Weinland suggests, "As you look out over a landscape, you note certain outstanding features—a river, a mountain, a railway, a red roof, a tall factory chimney. If you remember the scene, it will be by recalling these 'high spots.' In learning any kind of subject matter, it is necessary to concentrate on the high spots, the most significant things."[2]

To help you remember the path you have taken, look back over all twelve chapters. Record the high spots you discovered—the vistas of truth, the hidden vales of gratitude, the tranquil streams of conviction. Choose the things you want to remember and act upon.

Who Is This Jesus? _____

_____

_____

_____

Christ Is Raised, but What about Me? _____

_____

_____

_____

2. James D. Weinland, *How to Improve Your Memory* (New York, N.Y.: Barnes and Noble, 1957), p. 49.

How Can I Win Over Worry? _____

_____

_____

_____

What's Necessary for Victory? _____

_____

_____

_____

Is My Neighbor Really Lost? _____

_____

_____

_____

What Makes a Rebel Return? _____

_____

_____

_____

Can "Ordinary People" Make a Contribution? _____

_____

_____

_____

Will You Lead or Lag? _____

_____

_____

_____

Why Are We So Blessed? _____

_____

_____

_____

What Is My Response to God's Blessings? _____

_____

_____   _____

_____

How Should We Interpret God's Calendar? _____

_____

_____

_____

Why Do We Throw Rocks at Each Other? _____

_____

_____

_____

BOOKS FOR
PROBING FURTHER

We have covered a lot of territory in this series of questions! From the basic issue of who Jesus is to the complex issues of rebellion and stewardship, we've encountered a number of topics that perplex many Christians.

We hope this study has shed some light on a path that is sometimes hard to see. For further illumination, here are some books that will open your eyes to new vistas and keep your vision steady when problems threaten to lead you astray.

Bruce, F. F. *Jesus: Lord and Savior.* Downers Grove, Ill.: InterVarsity Press, 1986. The world offers many theories about who Jesus is— everything from a prophet to a liar to a good moral teacher. But F. F. Bruce offers more than theories; he gives us answers based on the truth of Scripture and goes one step further to tell us what implications those answers hold for us.

Little, Paul E. *How to Give Away Your Faith.* Downers Grove, Ill.: InterVarsity Press, 1966. Many Christians feel frustrated because they want to share their faith but don't know how to go about it. This book emphasizes instruction rather than exhortation and presents practical suggestions for reaching your world for Christ.

Minirth, Frank B., and Paul D. Meier. *Happiness Is a Choice.* Grand Rapids, Mich.: Baker Book House, 1978. It's confusing and disappointing when our faith in God doesn't seem to overcome our negative emotions. The authors combine their professional training, counseling experience, and biblical knowledge to give us an easy-to-follow guide for dealing with depression.

Pache, René. *The Future Life.* Chicago, Ill.: Moody Press, 1962. One of the founders of InterVarsity Christian Fellowship, Dr. René Pache discusses issues that baffle even mature believers. He gives clear, biblical information on such topics as death, the world of spirits, the resurrection, eternal perdition, and heaven.

Stafford, Tim. *Knowing the Face of God.* Grand Rapids, Mich.: Zondervan Publishing House, 1986. There is no deeper human longing than to know God. Yet, even as Christians, we often feel frustrated in the attempt. Tim Stafford shares his own search for the means to knowing God, and in the process, challenges us to begin that quest for ourselves.

Swindoll, Charles R. *Growing Deep in the Christian Life.* Portland, Oreg.: Multnomah Press, 1986. Doctrine and theology are such lofty topics that only seminary professors seem equipped for the climb. But it's important for all Christians to scale the peaks for themselves. In this practical book on theology, you will be given a foothold on Christianity's greatest truths, which are put into words that are easy to understand and enjoy.

————. *Hand Me Another Brick.* Nashville, Tenn.: Thomas Nelson Publishers, 1978. With principles taken from the story of Nehemiah, this book shows how to overcome discouragement and apply the spiritual "bricks" of motivation to yourself and others.

————. *Improving Your Serve.* Waco, Tex.: Word Books, 1981. Jesus asks us to be servants, but we live in a world that tells us to look out for number one. This conflict prompted Chuck to do a two-year investigation on the subject of servanthood, and this book is the result of that study.

White, John. *Parents in Pain.* Downers Grove, Ill.: InterVarsity Press, 1979. There are few things more heartbreaking than the rebellion of your own child. Although the author does offer practical suggestions for particular situations, he writes primarily to help parents cope with their own sense of guilt, frustration, anger, and inadequacy.

NOTES

NOTES

NOTES

NOTES

Insight for Living
Cassette Tapes
QUESTIONS CHRISTIANS ASK

Our steps to salvation and our journey along the path of faith are often punctuated by experiences and discoveries that cause us to question the direction we are heading. These questions are some of life's most crucial, because they relate to the very foundation of our relationship with God. Here's a study that examines a dozen of these crucial questions. By turning to the Scriptures, we will find answers that strengthen our walk with God. In the process, we will also find ourselves being drawn closer to Him.

			U.S.	Canada
QCA	CS	Cassette series—includes album cover ..	$34.50	$43.75
		Individual cassettes—include messages A and B	5.00	6.35

These prices are subject to change without notice.

QCA 1-A: *Who Is This Jesus?*—Matthew 21:1–17
   B: *Christ Is Raised, but What about Me?*—
       1 Corinthians 15:12–57

QCA 2-A: *How Can I Win Over Worry?*—Luke 10:38–42,
       Isaiah 40:27–31, Matthew 6:24–34, Philippians 4:4–7
   B: *What's Necessary for Victory?*—Romans 8:31–37;
       1 Corinthians 9:24–27; 1 John 5:4, 7

QCA 3-A: *Is My Neighbor Really Lost?*—Luke 10:25–37
   B: *What Makes a Rebel Return?*—Selected Scripture

QCA 4-A: *Can "Ordinary People" Make a Contribution?*—
       Acts 8–9
   B: *Will You Lead or Lag?*—1 Corinthians 14:33,
       Exodus 18

QCA 5-A: *Why Are We So Blessed?*—Psalms 103, 67
   B: *What Is My Response to God's Blessings?*—
       Matthew 25:14–30

QCA 6-A: *How Should We Interpret God's Calendar?*—
       Matthew 24:3–14
   B: *Why Do We Throw Rocks at Each Other?*—
       Ephesians 4:25–32

107

How to Order by Mail

Simply mark on the order form whether you want the series or individual tapes. Mail the form with your payment to the appropriate address listed below. We will process your order as promptly as we can.

United States: Mail your order to the Sales Department at Insight for Living, Post Office Box 4444, Fullerton, California 92634. If you wish your order to be shipped first-class for faster delivery, add 10 percent of the total order amount (not including California sales tax). Otherwise, please allow four to six weeks for delivery by fourth-class mail. We accept personal checks, money orders, Visa, or MasterCard in payment for materials. Unfortunately, we are unable to offer invoicing or COD orders.

Canada: Mail your order to Insight for Living Ministries, Post Office Box 2510, Vancouver, British Columbia V6B 3W7. Please add 7 percent of your total order for first-class postage and allow approximately four weeks for delivery. Our listeners in British Columbia must also add a 6 percent sales tax to the total of all tape orders (not including postage). We accept personal checks, money orders, Visa, or MasterCard in payment for materials. Unfortunately, we are unable to offer invoicing or COD orders.

Australia, New Zealand, or Papua New Guinea: Mail your order to Insight for Living, Inc., GPO Box 2823 EE, Melbourne, Victoria 3001, Australia. Please allow six to ten weeks for delivery by surface mail. If you would like your order sent airmail, the delivery time may be reduced. Whether you choose surface or airmail, postage costs must be added to the amount of purchase and included with your order. Please use the chart that follows to determine correct postage. Due to fluctuating currency rates, we can accept only personal checks made payable in U.S. funds, international money orders, Visa, or MasterCard in payment for materials.

Overseas: Other overseas residents should contact our U.S. office. Please allow six to ten weeks for delivery by surface mail. If you would like your order sent airmail, the delivery time may be reduced. Whether you choose surface or airmail, postage costs must be added to the amount of purchase and included with your order. Please use the chart that follows to determine correct postage. Due to fluctuating currency rates, we can accept only personal checks made payable in U.S. funds, international money orders, Visa, or MasterCard in payment for materials.

Type of Postage	Postage Cost
Surface	10% of total order
Airmail	25% of total order

For Faster Service, Order by Telephone

To purchase using Visa or MasterCard, you are welcome to use our toll-free numbers between the hours of 8:30 A.M. and 4:00 P.M., Pacific time, Monday through Friday. The number to call from anywhere in the United States is **1-800-772-8888.** To order from Canada, call our Vancouver office at **1-800-663-7639.** Vancouver residents should call (604) 272-5811. Telephone orders from overseas are handled through our Sales Department at (714) 870-9161. We are unable to accept collect calls.

Our Guarantee

Our cassettes are guaranteed for ninety days against faulty performance or breakage due to a defect in the tape. For best results, please be sure your tape recorder is in good operating condition and is cleaned regularly.

Note: To cover processing and handling, there is a $10 fee for *any* returned check.

Order Form

QCA CS represents the entire *Questions Christians Ask* series, while QCA 1–6 are the individual tapes included in the series.

Series or Tape	Unit Price U.S.	Canada	Quantity	Amount
QCA CS	$34.50	$43.75		$
QCA 1	5.00	6.35		
QCA 2	5.00	6.35		
QCA 3	5.00	6.35		
QCA 4	5.00	6.35		
QCA 5	5.00	6.35		
QCA 6	5.00	6.35		
			Subtotal	
	Sales tax 6% for orders delivered in California or British Columbia			
	Postage 7% in Canada; overseas residents see "How to Order by Mail"			
	10% optional first-class shipping and handling U.S. residents only			
	Gift to Insight for Living Tax-deductible in the U.S. and Canada			
	Total amount due Please do not send cash.			$

If there is a balance: ☐ apply it as a donation ☐ please refund

Form of payment:

☐ Check or money order made payable to Insight for Living

☐ Credit card (circle one):   Visa   MasterCard

Card Number _____ Expiration Date _____

Signature _____
We cannot process your credit card purchase without your signature.

Name _____

Address _____

City _____

State/Province_____ Zip/Postal Code _____

Country _____

Telephone __(____)_____ Radio Station ____ ____ ____ ____
If questions arise concerning your order, we may need to contact you.

Mail this order form to the Sales Department at one of these addresses:
Insight for Living, Post Office Box 4444, Fullerton, CA 92634
Insight for Living Ministries, Post Office Box 2510, Vancouver, BC, Canada V6B 3W7
Insight for Living, Inc., GPO Box 2823 EE, Melbourne, VIC 3001, Australia

Order Form

QCA CS represents the entire *Questions Christians Ask* series, while QCA 1–6 are the individual tapes included in the series.

Series or Tape	Unit Price U.S.	Canada	Quantity	Amount
QCA CS	$34.50	$43.75		$
QCA 1	5.00	6.35		
QCA 2	5.00	6.35		
QCA 3	5.00	6.35		
QCA 4	5.00	6.35		
QCA 5	5.00	6.35		
QCA 6	5.00	6.35		
Subtotal				
Sales tax *6% for orders delivered in California or British Columbia*				
Postage *7% in Canada; overseas residents see "How to Order by Mail"*				
10% optional first-class shipping and handling *U.S. residents only*				
Gift to Insight for Living *Tax-deductible in the U.S. and Canada*				
Total amount due *Please do not send cash.*				$

If there is a balance: ☐ apply it as a donation ☐ please refund

Form of payment:

☐ Check or money order made payable to Insight for Living

☐ Credit card (circle one):   Visa   MasterCard

Card Number _____ Expiration Date _____

Signature _____
We cannot process your credit card purchase without your signature.

Name _____

Address _____

City _____

State/Province_____ Zip/Postal Code _____

Country _____

Telephone __(____)_____ Radio Station ____ ____ ____ ____
If questions arise concerning your order, we may need to contact you.

Mail this order form to the Sales Department at one of these addresses:
Insight for Living, Post Office Box 1111, Fullerton, CA 92634
Insight for Living Ministries, Post Office Box 2510, Vancouver, BC, Canada V6B 3W7
Insight for Living, Inc., GPO Box 2823 EE, Melbourne, VIC 3001, Australia

Order Form

QCA CS represents the entire *Questions Christians Ask* series, while QCA 1–6 are the individual tapes included in the series.

Series or Tape	Unit Price U.S.	Canada	Quantity	Amount
QCA CS	$34.50	$43.75		$
QCA 1	5.00	6.35		
QCA 2	5.00	6.35		
QCA 3	5.00	6.35		
QCA 4	5.00	6.35		
QCA 5	5.00	6.35		
QCA 6	5.00	6.35		
			Subtotal	
			Sales tax 6% for orders delivered in California or British Columbia	
			Postage 7% in Canada; overseas residents see "How to Order by Mail"	
			10% optional first-class shipping and handling U.S. residents only	
			Gift to Insight for Living Tax-deductible in the U.S. and Canada	
			Total amount due Please do not send cash.	$

If there is a balance: ☐ apply it as a donation ☐ please refund

Form of payment:

☐ Check or money order made payable to Insight for Living

☐ Credit card (circle one):   Visa   MasterCard

    Card Number _____ Expiration Date _____

    Signature _____
             We cannot process your credit card purchase without your signature.

Name _____

Address _____

City _____

State/Province_____ Zip/Postal Code _____

Country _____

Telephone __(____)_____ Radio Station ____ ____ ____ ____
       If questions arise concerning your order, we may need to contact you.

Mail this order form to the Sales Department at one of these addresses:
Insight for Living, Post Office Box 4444, Fullerton, CA 92634
Insight for Living Ministries, Post Office Box 2510, Vancouver, BC, Canada V6B 3W7
Insight for Living, Inc., GPO Box 2823 EE, Melbourne, VIC 3001, Australia